Everyday spaces

The potential of neighbourhood space

Pauline Gallacher

ThomasTelford

Published by Thomas Telford Publishing, Thomas Telford Ltd, 1 Heron Quay, London E14 4JD. www.thomastelford.com

Distributors for Thomas Telford books are
USA: ASCE Press, 1801 Alexander Bell Drive, Reston, VA 20191-4400, USA
Japan: Maruzen Co. Ltd, Book Department, 3–10 Nihonbashi 2-chome, Chuo-ku, Tokyo 103
Australia: DA Books and Journals, 648 Whitehorse Road, Mitcham 3132, Victoria

First published 2005

Cover photos: Huntly Town Square, Aberdeenshire (front) and disused abattoir, Glasgow © Pauline Gallacher; Five Spaces, Glasgow (Saracen opening) © Alan Dimmick; Community playground, Drumchapel (front) © Louise Crawford and Stephan Gueneau

A catalogue record for this book is available from the British Library

ISBN: 0 7277 3344 3

Typeset by Jack Andrews Design
Printed and bound in Great Britain by CUP

In memory of my parents, who gave us space to live.

ACKNOWLEDGEMENTS

Ken Worpole

Rob Cowan

Professor Jan Gehl

Alastair Haines, Rick Hall and Venu Dhupa, NESTA

Stuart MacDonald

Eleanor McAllister

The Five Spaces housing associations staff and management committees

Jon Rouse and David Harding for comments on the draft

Glasgow City Council

NESTA, the National Endowment for Science, Technology and the Arts for Fellowship funding and contributions towards publication

Images

Ken and Larraine Worpole: Figs. 1–12

Alan Dimmick: Figs. 2.2, 2.4, 2.6, 2.7, 2.10, 2.12–2.17, 2.23, 2.25, 2.26, 2.31, 2.33–2.36, 2.40, 6.1–6.3

Andrew Lee Photography: Figs. 2.3, 2.11, 2.24, 2.32, 2.41

Brian Evans: Figs. 2.8, 2.28, 2.29

Zoo Architects: Fig. 3.3

Ateneu Nou Barris: Fig. 4.12

Roisin McCloskey: Fig. 5.5

Adrian Stewart: Fig. 6.8

Rob Cowan: Fig. 7.2

Stephen Healy: Fig. 7.7

Dan Dubowitz: Fig. 7.8

All others by Pauline Gallacher

Maps

© Neil Baxter Associates/Glasgow City Council

CONTENTS

INTRODUCTION BY URBAN DESIGN GROUP

'It's hard to design a space that will not attract people,' wrote the celebrated urbanist and sociologist William 'Holly' Whyte. 'What is remarkable is how often this has been accomplished.'

Glasgow's Five Spaces project was a determined attempt to learn from some of those past failures. The project brought together talented designers and artists, planners, engineers, local residents and generous budgets to create public spaces, not in a town or city centre, but in the places where people live. Surely such a combination would produce results worthy of a City of Architecture and Design? But the outcome was only a partial success.

Reading this book in draft, we at the Urban Design Group were struck by how unusual it was. Here was someone who had been intimately involved in a series of urban design projects reviewing the experience with disarming frankness and great insight. Pauline Gallacher not only spells out the lessons of Glasgow's experience, but also asks the tricky questions on which creating successful spaces depends.

Is it even realistic to expect to create civic space in residential neighbourhoods? Does public space have meaning in the privatised, globalised, 21st century – or has civic life been so much diminished that it no longer needs a physical expression? Is there any real chance of designers, artists, planners, engineers and local residents collaborating successfully when they all see the world in such different ways?

Everyday spaces makes a great contribution to showing what processes might help us make sense of urban complexity. Learning that there is no single profession with simple solutions has itself been a step forward. As the great urbanist Patrick Geddes wrote a hundred years ago: 'A city is more than a place in space. It is a drama in time.' Pauline Gallacher is a critic of rare insight.

Rob Cowan
Director, Urban Design Group

FOREWORD

There is today a great deal of interest in the renewal of public space and public life. Much of this interest has its roots in the 1960s and early 1970s, when architects, planners and politicians – following growing public disquiet – realised that certain kinds of over-rationalised forms of urban planning were beginning to eradicate the more sociable aspects of street life and culture. Two names in particular spring to mind in this regard – William H. Whyte, working in and writing about New York and other North American cities, and Jan Gehl, Professor of Architecture at The Royal Danish Academy of Fine Arts in Copenhagen, working in conjunction with Copenhagen City Council. Both not only produced a string of books and studies about street life, but both were also similarly engaged in practical projects to restore forms of urban vitality to their city's respective streets and neighbourhoods.

Whyte's pioneering study, *The Social Life of Small Urban Spaces*, first published in 1980, employed time-lapse photography to show how people used every opportunity offered by a spot of fine weather to gather, sit, read, talk wherever there was a spare seat, bench, stoop or low boundary wall to do so. In his view, it was these kinds of human presences and transactions that made urban life bearable and even enjoyable. His influence reaches down into the heart of the contemporary organisation, the Project for Public Places, based in New York, of which he was a founder member (Figs. 1,2).

While Whyte's work concentrated on re-designing and programming a large number of discrete spaces in the city, Gehl's project in Copenhagen was much more strategic and ambitious. It was nothing less than a long-term initiative to re-shape the city's public life and culture from one largely based on indoor eating, drinking and leisure – partly due to the public's alienation from the increasingly car-dominated street scene – to one based on a outdoor 'cafe culture', then more likely to be found in towns and cities in southern Europe and

Fig. 1.   Bryant Park, New York. An early success story for the idea of turning a failed public space around, from a place of fear to a place of urban conviviality

Fig. 2.   Battery Park, New York. A new linear park along the west side of Manhattan, now a popular meeting place and pedestrian boulevard

the Mediterranean. Gehl's analysis of what had gone wrong is contained in his book, *Life Between Buildings: Using Public Space*, first published in 1980, and his account of the highly successful programme to re-invent Copenhagen's street life and culture is to be found in *Public Spaces, Public Life*, written with Lars Gemzøe and published in 1996. This latter publication is indispensable to the contemporary urbanist or planner (Figs. 3,4).

The British incentive to re-think the role of public spaces came with the creation of an Urban Task Force in 1998, the year after the election of the New Labour government, and whose report, *Towards an Urban Renaissance*, was published in 1999. This was strongly influenced by Barcelona's success in creating new public spaces in that city – indeed, the Foreword to the Urban Task Force report was written by Pasqual Maragell, former Mayor of Barcelona. In Pauline Gallacher's evaluation that follows, Barcelona's example was equally iconic for Glasgow's Millennium Spaces Project, and Gallacher interestingly seeks to understand why this was so and to such a large degree (Figs. 5,6).

Since 1999, a number of studies, reports and initiatives have flowed from the UK government on these issues, including:

■ the Select Committee Report, *Town and Country Parks* (1999)

■ *The Urban White Paper* (2001)

■ *PPG 17: Public Spaces* (2002)

■ the Urban Green Spaces Task Force Report, *Green Spaces, Better Places* (2002)

■ the Office of the Deputy Prime Minister Report, *Living Places: Cleaner, Safer, Greener* (2002)

■ *Sustainable Communities: An Action Programme* (2003).

A dedicated 'Space Unit' devoted to these issues was established at CABE (Commission for Architecture and the Built Environment) in May 2003. Lottery funding has been

awarded to a number of ambitious and successful plans to re-make city centre public space, including Birmingham's refurbished Victoria Square (Fig. 7), Sheffield's Peace Gardens (Fig. 8) and Newcastle's new urban square adjacent to the Laing Art Gallery, designed by Thomas Heatherwick (Fig. 9).

Much of this new energy and funding has concentrated on city centre sites and projects, but the need at a neighbourhood level is just as urgent. For this reason, this book by Pauline Gallacher is particularly timely, even if some of its conclusions make challenging reading. Though the author is not sparing in her description of the problems that attended this ambitious initiative, the lessons to be learned from Glasgow's Year of Architecture Five Spaces project, will, I am sure, be appreciated and considered widely.

In addition to the issues raised by Pauline Gallacher in her study, I would highlight some of the following as being of particular concern to local politicians, housing providers, architects and designers elsewhere, as the commitment to

Fig. 3. Nyhavn, Copenhagen. A former run-down waterfront, now one of the liveliest gathering places in Northern Europe

Fig. 4. Strøget, the main shopping street in Copenhagen, and a pioneering example of the successfully pedestrianised city centre

Fig. 5. Parc de l'Espanya Industriel, Barcelona, one of the bold designs for a new generation of public spaces commissioned and constructed between 1981 and 1997

Fig. 6. A new pier or maritime boulevard in Barcelona, the Rambla de Mar, which continues the famous Ramblas out to a new shopping and leisure complex at Port Vell, completed in 1994

Fig. 7. Victoria Square, Birmingham, one of the re-designed public spaces linked together to restore the city centre to the pedestrian

Fig. 8. The new Peace Gardens in Sheffield, directly adjacent to the Victorian town hall, now a popular meeting place

Fig. 3

Fig. 4

Fig. 5

Fig. 6

Fig. 7

Fig. 8

Fig. 9

Fig. 10

Fig. 11

Fig. 12

providing 'cleaner, safer, greener' streets and public spaces in Britain's towns and cities gathers momentum.

■ Particular problems arise when it is assumed that housing alone provides the principal material basis of 'community', when it clearly doesn't. Without churches, schools, shops, parks, libraries and voluntary networks of association such as clubs and societies – as well as some local services providing employment – then it is very difficult to say that 'community' in any meaningful way exists at all. So, as well as a built community there has to be an associational community and an economic community. Without local economic networks offering the opportunities for the exchange of goods and services, then a neighbourhood begins to become a dependency, cut off from the economic flows and opportunities of the wider society.

■ It is not surprising that the most successful new public spaces are associated with 'mixed use' economies and settings: places where shoppers, schoolchildren, workers off-duty, visitors, tourists, and others brush against each other in the course of pursuing their different timetables, but gaining something intangible from each other's presence on the street, or in the park, walking, sitting on a bench eating a sandwich or smoking a cigarette. The use

Fig. 9.   The 'Blue Carpet' in Newcastle, a new public space designed by architect Thomas Heatherwick, made of crushed glass, and completed in 2002

Fig. 10.   The design that failed. An early photograph of the re-design of the northern end of Museumpark in Rotterdam, by OMA (Office for Metropolitan Architecture), completed in 1994, conceptualised as an apple orchard planted in a bed of seashells

Fig. 11.   Lack of maintenance and vandalism quickly caused the Museumpark in Rotterdam to deteriorate

Fig. 12.   By 2001 the Museumpark was levelled flat: an expensive lesson in getting the balance right between concept, care and appropriate uses

of the car has bitten deeply into these forms of street life in many places, but they can and do survive in many others.

■ Further to this basic connection of new public space to local economic vibrancy, it is worth remembering the words of the American urban designer Alexander Garvin who once wrote: 'Urban planning should be defined as public action that will produce a sustained and widespread private market reaction.' That is to say, if any new public space is not designed without some conscious thought given to increasing human activity and exchange, as well as adding to the economic value of local neighbourhoods and facilities, then it is likely to fail.

■ Given the deep social and economic nature of the circumstances that so frequently underpin or undermine a vibrant community and public space culture, it is clear that design or architecture alone cannot solve these problems, though in many places there is still a pretence that they can. As this book demonstrates, the success stories in the Five Spaces project happened where the community already felt it had something going for it anyway, and also had a strong sense of its own identity and power to change. Some also question why it is still assumed that artists in particular should enjoy a privileged status with regard to the design of public spaces, given that the history of public art itself has been fraught with problems and failures. The contribution of artists can be enormously beneficial, but it needs to be tempered with a degree of local knowledge and cold-blooded good sense. Glasgow is not alone in now requiring a public art de-commissioning programme, examining which works in which places are now deemed to have failed or outlived their usefulness and become a maintenance and aesthetic liability.

■ Even where significant artwork and good design did happen, and was appreciated, then a failure to agree on the responsibility and appropriate levels of funding for maintenance sometimes meant that only months further down the line, the important achievements were already being compromised and the project was set on the road to decline. It is increasingly said that the British, compared with the rest of Europe, are very good at designing things and creating fine architecture, but terrible at maintaining them. Even so, failures of an even bigger magnitude have happened elsewhere, as shown in the rapid and sad decline of Rotterdam's prestigious Museumpark. (Figs. 10–12)

■ It is also transparently clear from this study that new skills are needed if we are to begin to develop responsive and dedicated forms of public space management and maintenance. The fact that any kind of water or non-standard lighting feature now poses insoluble problems for public maintenance (this story can be repeated throughout almost every parks service in the UK) is sorry testimony to the minimalist repair culture now prevalent.

■ Finally, this book also points out the dilemmas involved in creating a new culture of public space vitality and culture, and in finding a balance between local forms of ownership and control (usually without proper funding), or more centralised forms of management and maintenance (which may be better placed to attract the funding, but does not possess the local knowledge and pride of place which comes with the territory). Clearly, each town and city will have to find its own solution, negotiated locally.

Having now read through this work several times on different occasions, each reading brings forward new thoughts, ideas and insights. It is very rich indeed, and, though disheartening at times in the stories it tells, is nevertheless also passionate about its subject matter and the belief that things can be done better in the future – and deserve to be.

Ken Worpole

Ken Worpole acted as mentor to Pauline Gallacher on this NESTA project, and is the author of a number of books and studies on the urban public domain.

INTRODUCTION

In his foreword, Ken Worpole offered a critical snapshot of the significance and investment accorded to public space in European cities. It has long been the complaint of landscape and urban design professionals that the UK is the poor relation in this regard. This is now changing, of course, and there has been an explosion of policy making and critical writing on the subject.

What follows (Chapters 1 to 4) is an account of a particular project, unique for its time. It reveals a general lack of focus on the issue of public space in ordinary neighbourhoods, in contrast to the increasing amount of attention devoted to city centre locations. This is beginning to change. More specifically, it points to an intriguing gap in thinking around what may be called neighbourhood *civic* spaces – the special, extraordinary episodes that help define an area to itself and to others. What might these spaces be in 21st century neighbourhoods? Are they relevant at all?

Chapter 5 takes a broader view, placing these special interventions in the context of the unremarkable, the everyday and local, where, arguably, a consideration of the subject would have begun, had not the Five Spaces dictated the shape of this study.

Chapter 6 proposes a method by which the ambition to create special places may form an integral part of a wider investigation into the nature of neighbourhood identity, one which addresses the more functional and modest spaces *at the same time*. The general approach is that *cultural work* is a necessary condition for delivering the greatest value (long and short term) for local people out of place-making projects and for achieving high-quality physical solutions that are appropriate, 'owned' and integrated.

Doing the work in this order (from the particular and special to the general and ordinary) has been useful in that it has required speculation beyond the programmatic and functional to the deeper issues that lie embedded in something so literally pedestrian as the streets outside our doors. To claim this significance for everyday space is not to imply that every kerbside should be saturated with embellishment, but to recognise that all external space, from the school gate to the war memorial, combines to offer a palette of opportunities for the enrichment of our common life.

Chapter 1

From Barcelona to Possilpark: Five Spaces for Glasgow

SUMMARY

The Five Spaces initiative (Fig. 1.1) was one of the three main capital projects of Glasgow, UK City of Architecture and Design 1999[1]. It was a highly ambitious project that left the city with new urban spaces in neighbourhoods that could not otherwise have aspired to such provision. Funders recognised its importance in their willingness to back the scheme, notwithstanding its inherent difficulties. The Five Spaces were delivered in an innovative process that saw artists working as full members of the individual design teams, with local community-based housing associations as clients.

Local ownership was one of the project's core ideas. In the following, the projects are described, in terms of their origins and current condition, in the context of a series of evaluatory conversations with the housing association participants.

THE VISION

The Five Spaces, or Millennium Spaces project, is probably thought of as a creature of the Glasgow 1999 Festival. And so it was, but its origins predate the 1999 process. A tentative attempt had been made by the city's community-based housing association movement, under the auspices of its training organisation SHARE (Scottish Housing Associations Resources for Education), to muster support for such a project. The idea was to lever Lottery funds into some of the poorer areas of the city, reaching parts of the urban fabric and in a way that was beyond the means of the funders of urban regeneration at that time. With the advent of 'Glasgow 1999', the capacity to advance the project was available and it fitted very well with the aspirations of the 1999 programme.

The project was highly ambitious in terms of both process and product. Its inspiration was the public spaces programme in Barcelona, which had seen over 100 such projects inserted into the dense urban mass of the city, opening it up but also signalling a process of revitalisation that was to receive a

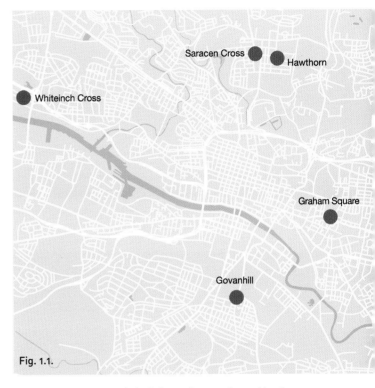

Fig. 1.1.

Fig. 1.1. Location of Whiteinch Cross, Saracen Cross, Hawthorn, Graham Square and Govanhill

massive boost with the Olympics[2]. The Barcelona initiative was not part of an integrated regeneration programme. Housing, a major problem in the inner city, was not in the remit of the City Council. Nevertheless, the programme was strategic and egalitarian: better places for the entire city, good for local people and for the messages it sent out to the wider world. It understood that place is an important generator of confidence, identity and wider investment. So, if the context was very different, what could be taken from the scheme was its élan, its vision, its willingness to try different approaches, the belief that what happens in between buildings can be a major contributor to the quality of life for local people. And its willingness to make bold design moves, many of which worked brilliantly, others less so.

What Glasgow had in *its* favour was the possibility of making a contribution to an urban redevelopment process that was already in full swing. Like Barcelona, Glasgow could not offer a seamless integration of spaces and surrounding development; community-based housing regeneration had been going for 25 years. But even in situations where the majority of development decisions had already been made, the past absence of masterplanning and lack of substantial funds for open spaces had meant that there were many leftover spaces that both detracted from the investment made in housing and had negative impact on quality of life.

Even more significant would be the intended procurement process by which these spaces were delivered. The role of the community-based housing associations in area regeneration was already well established. Some of them had increasingly developed ambitions with regard to housing design. It was assumed there would be a willingness to embrace the challenge of developing the idea of public space, away from the necessarily limited scope of streetscaping programmes, which was all that was on offer (if at all). So, realising that process was vital to the delivery of schemes appropriate to local circumstances, and given that the project had its earliest beginnings in the movement,

the housing associations were from the start seen as both client and conduit of community ownership.

THE CHALLENGES

The vagaries of funding setbacks and the difficulties that the resultant cutbacks produced in terms of specification and delivery might now only be unpleasant memories for those who struggled to produce the projects on time for the festival year, but they were also major influences on what was produced and the way in which it was delivered. What was designed as an innovative and ambitious process had to be accommodated as well as possible to the imperative of having the spaces delivered during 1999. The challenges, therefore, were many:

- to deliver the whole programme for 1999
- to retain the ambition of the project
- to manage a depleted budget
- to manage the design teams within each project, in which a new type of collaboration was being set up between artists, landscape designers and architects
- to ensure that each housing association (HA) had client control while, as it turned out, running the project on a co-ordinated construction management basis
- to ensure that each project was well communicated to its local audience
- to maximise the learning opportunities for local children afforded by the process
- to ensure the sustainability of the project in the long term.

In the midst of these at times conflicting values, it was easy – and has been in retrospect – to lose sight of what the project was essentially about.

- It was to be an exemplar – not in the sense of having resolved every detail, but in the sense of trying something new and having good reasons for doing it.

Fig. 1.2.

Fig. 1.2.   Learning from Barcelona. Residents, students, planners and architects visit the public spaces together

■ It was offered to the city as a starting point for a debate about the role of public space in neighbourhoods such as these, and how best to make them and manage them.

MAKING IT HAPPEN: THE INDUCTION PROCESS

From the outset, the project was seen to be innovatory, and the induction process was designed to harness the twin values of ambitious design and local ownership.

Barcelona

The project got off to an inspirational start with a visit to Barcelona for a combined party of housing association committee members, architects and planners (Fig. 1.2). For many it was not only their first visit to the city but was also the first time they had confronted the idea of urban space as an issue in its own right. It was not only what people saw that was important, but that they saw it together – the debate between professionals and non-professionals could take place naturally and on neutral territory.

The Briggait

In June 1996, design professionals, students and the prospective clients came together to look at site information and photos, make comments and listen to a range of contributors from city officials to Enric Miralles (a Catalan architect, designer of the Scottish Parliament Building, who died during the project) (Fig. 1.3). Twenty housing associations, co-ops, one residents' association and a conservation trust responded to the invitation to bring forward

Fig. 1.3

Fig. 1.4

Fig. 1.3. Enric Miralles at the first Glasgow Spaces workshop, June 1996

Fig. 1.4. A major two-day event in Glasgow School of Art with community clients, artists and designers, September 1996

sites and aspirations to the inaugural, open event in a converted market.

Glasgow School of Art

A two-day intensive event brought people closer to the specific challenges of their own sites, in the auspicious surroundings of C. R. Mackintosh's masterpiece, the Glasgow School of Art (Fig. 1.4). Despite many years in the business of being HA clients, for many it was their first experience of seeing designers at work, sharing the process of site visits, studio conversations around the drawing board and, newest of all, the contributions of artists to the design team. Sharing space with so many diverse teams and projects allowed the transmission of ideas between one project to another as relationships were formed. As an approach to commissioning it was certainly beyond the experience of the associations; the explosion of creative energy (not just from the designers) made for a memorable experience. There was plenty of time thereafter to formalise arrangements and sort out all the practical aspects.

PROJECT SELECTION

The final number of individual projects delivered emerged from a process of elimination based on site potential, funding eligibility and deliverability. A steering group selected the 15 most promising sites, which were the subject of an unsuccessful application to the Millennium Commission. This list was finally reduced to five – a complicated enough task.

THE STRUGGLE FOR FUNDING

Without an exhaustive trawl though funding and project correspondence, it would be difficult to comment in detail on the web of relationships and events that defined the design process as it transpired. The project had a long gestation, principally due to funding difficulties. Applications were made

to the Millennium Commission, the European Regional Development Fund, the Scottish Arts Council (SAC) Lottery and Scottish Homes[3]. The SAC was, from the outset, most supportive of the idea. Making it fit their assessment criteria was another matter. The final funding package comprised the Scottish Arts Council, Scottish Homes (the majority funder) and Glasgow City Council in the shape of year 1999 staff time and commitment to maintenance. Europe came to the rescue of the Hawthorn space with its URBAN programme. There was a long period when the process was on hold, when extensive work by consultants and clients was not justifiable in terms of professional time and raised community expectations. Then suddenly, it seemed, the project was finally funded, albeit with a reduced budget, and the pressure was on to deliver.

It may be said that these difficulties matter little in the eye of history but it is worth giving a little more space to what happened at the time. A fundamental principle of the SAC Lottery application was that projects should not commence before approval was given. Because the arts component was, properly, inextricable from the rest of the scheme, it was not possible, even if desirable, for the designs to be well advanced at application stage. The whole basis of the project, after all, was that it should be process-led. But funders have a legitimate right to know what they are funding, so there emerged a negotiation that required an increasing degree of specificity, in terms of both cost and design. Everyone involved was new to projects of this scale and ambition. Meanwhile the 1999 countdown ticked inexorably on. Inevitably there were compromises in the struggle to render the project worthy of support and capable of delivery.

DELIVERY: THE CONSTRUCTION MANAGEMENT APPROACH

As the complexities of each project became more apparent, to say nothing of their diminishing budgets, it was decided to adopt a novel approach to the business of delivery. A firm of construction managers was brought in (also involved in the realisation of Homes for the Future, a major 1999 project). It was charged with liaison with the five separate design teams and their clients, assembling the whole project into a deliverable shape and progressing the applications to the satisfaction of the funders. The construction management approach operated over four of the five sites, enabling works and materials packages to be devised with resultant economies of scale and cost control. (The fifth, Graham Square, was procured by a different route.) An intermediate labour market programme, Glasgow Works, was also integrated into the scheme; this resulted in 23 long-term unemployed people being given training for work and a programme of self-development. The majority of these went on into full employment. The projects were delivered on time and to budget – no small feat in such a complex programme. Inevitably, though, there were costs in terms of the clients' perception of their roles. These are discussed further in Chapter 3.

DEFECTS PERIOD AND HANDOVER

Four projects were completed during 1999. The last, Graham Square, had to await the completion of the housing projects around it, but all were showcased in a dedicated publication [1] and other Glasgow 1999 material.

Every scheme had its own hard and soft landscaping defects periods, most of which ran well into 2000 and even 2001. Each was then subject to scrutiny by the Land Services department of the City Council before being handed over for maintenance by them.

The situation with regard to *maintenance* was as follows. As part of the funding application process, written undertakings had to be made for the future maintenance of the spaces. Since the projects were almost totally on land owned by the council, and since the HAs had no formal remit and no funds in the matter, it fell to the council to indicate its willingness to adopt the spaces. With this in mind, council officers scrutinised the project designs and advised adjustments in specification. Land Services also made clear that it was not in a position to maintain 'special features' such as Whiteinch's 'waterwall' and the specialised artworks – the HAs, it seemed, would have to step into the breach. However, they in turn insisted they had no funds to do this on a long-term basis. *The matter was never resolved,* leaving a grey area that was bound to be problematic. Even as the defects period was underway there began to be problems of vandalism in some of the spaces, and a programme of works additional to the making good of defects was undertaken by the 1999 Company, under the supervision of the construction managers. The understanding was that, notwithstanding the issue of the artworks, the general maintenance situation was clear. The 1999 Company was finally wound up.

Chapter 2

Case study: Looking again at the Five Spaces, 1999–2002

INTRODUCTION

Post-occupancy evaluation is much recommended, but rarely practised. The award of a Fellowship from NESTA[4] has allowed an in-depth consideration of the Five Spaces, their ambitions, and how they have fared in the years since completion.

During late 2001 and early 2002 representatives of four of the five association committees were interviewed[5], and all of the spaces have been visited many times since then. An exhaustive questionnaire was sent to each association, and staff were asked to issue this to committee members as a way of structuring round-table conversations, which were recorded. The questionnaire covered all aspects of process, product and maintenance. All the responses are of interest, especially when we come to discuss how projects might be pursued in future. The issues of immediate relevance were clearly and urgently stated and are reported below.

The interviewees

The number of people who contributed to the reviews was very small. Left to the discretion of each housing association, the people who came along were all, with the exception of some attending at Hawthorn, closely involved with the Five Spaces project from the outset. These were people who had made the project their own, and although being far from blind to its shortcomings, identified themselves with it and were its champions, even within their own associations. Many of them had been on 'Design's on You'[6] courses before the Spaces project was conceived, and so perhaps had a more adventurous conception of their role as clients than others on their management committees. Several had then been on the study tour to Barcelona, and even in the interviews called on that experience to make their points. The interviews were thus neither scientific nor representative of HA committee views, and certainly not of the general public[7]. What they do offer are the reflections of those intimately involved, whose enthusiasm

for the endeavour has had to be tempered by the experience of having the projects as part of the local landscape, absorbing local comment into their own reflections on the process and product.

Other perspectives

In addition to the associations, the arts commissioning consultant, the construction manager, the deputy director of Glasgow 1999 and senior staff at Glasgow City Council Land Services were informally interviewed and their comments have contributed to the perspectives taken in this book. The architects and artists involved were not directly approached, partly due to the scale of this book, but, more importantly, to avoid too close a focus on the particularities of this or that space, the specification changes, the personality clashes and the timescales. These accounts would no doubt shed further light on the minutiae of what, how and why, but would contribute little to the central theme of this book: the place of small civic spaces such as this in the business of urban regeneration. Clearly, the designers will have reflections on this topic too, and their insights might be usefully called on in a larger work.

GOVANHILL

The client: Govanhill Housing Association Ltd

Govanhill is in the inner south side of Glasgow and is one of the city's most coherent remaining neighbourhoods of traditional sandstone tenement housing. The local community-based HA, one of Glasgow's first, has for more than 25 years restored, renewed and developed this area, moving from tenement improvement to newbuild and conversion of increasing ambition, to streetscaping and economic development. The creation of a community development trust is an example of how housing activity has

Fig. 2.1

Fig. 2.2

Fig. 2.3

Fig. 2.4

Fig. 2.1   Govanhill map
Fig. 2.2.   Govanhill: the site before
Fig. 2.3.   Govanhill: model
Fig. 2.4.   Govanhill: the completed scheme

evolved into a broader area regeneration role. It is also one of the city's biggest multicultural neighbourhoods.

The brief: a gateway to Govanhill

Govanhill is a distinct area with a very strong identity, but it suffered from a weakly defined point of entry on the approach from the city centre. In recognition of this, the association had already begun to explore ideas for a 'gateway to Govanhill', possibly involving the relocation of an arch from a recently demolished church. The association had already commissioned a firm of landscape architects to consider the space, and this company became part of the design team for the 1999 scheme.

The committee also wished to encourage more community-based celebrations of the area's rich cultural diversity. Another consideration was the recently completed neighbourhood park situated close by. Although relatively small, it had been planned with close community consultation involving the Land Services department of the council, and was already highly popular and full of activity. There was no need to duplicate such a provision; indeed, the call was for a complementary sort of space. The final component was the presence of a community education building actually within the chosen site, with its own committee of management and an assumed degree of ownership.

Govanhill was fortunate in having a three-month artist's residency with its chosen artist in advance of the formal commission for the space. This enabled relationships to be formed, introduced the association to the artist's practice and allowed the artist to root herself in the area from a temporary studio in an empty flat overlooking the space. Her understanding of the space contributed strongly to the overall conception.

The project

The idea was for a space that might be informally adopted by the community education centre, which had plans for a gardening club. The Millennium Hut, the deliberately enigmatic structure in the centre of the space, was thus artwork, treehouse and vertically stacked potting shed. While serving as a local landmark, it was intended to evoke more complex meanings, looking at the idea of a 'den' or secret place – a place that could become anything you wanted it to be (Figs. 2.5, 2.6).

Fig. 2.5

Fig. 2.6

Fig. 2.7

Fig. 2.5. Govanhill: the Millennium Hut: echoes of the typical Glasgow doocot (pigeon loft) in background

Fig. 2.6. Govanhill: the Hut reveals a vertical potting shed, garden 'library' and lookout post

Fig. 2.7. Govanhill: awnings were designed to provide shelter and scenery for temporary events (shown here the opening in 1999)

Fig. 2.8. Govanhill: finishes and detail previously reserved for the city centre

Fig. 2.8

The multicultural nature of the neighbourhood, it was hoped, might express itself in the use of the informal gathering and performance space, complete with awnings for occasional use (Fig. 2.7). In day-to-day usage, the space was intended to be a congenial route and casual seating area away from the more concentrated uses of the nearby Govanhill Park (Fig. 2.8). The flat and open nature of the site was moderated by grassy mounding to shield the space from the heavy traffic along Cathcart Road, and an abstract patterning of paving and planting was designed to both change with the seasons and play with light, particularly when seen from the surrounding flats.

The project revisited

For some time, while the space performed relatively well, its specific uses did not develop as hoped. Fortunately, this did not impact too harshly on the general survival of the space, since its everyday use, its location and the nature of Govanhill as a locality preserved it from obvious decline. However, the real potential of the space was not being realised – the Millennium Hut established itself as a landmark with no apparent use. Even the modest plan to erect a Christmas tree did not happen. The community education centre did not take up the garden idea as well as had been hoped. It was difficult to get the lamps on the luminaires replaced by the council. It was not used for communal celebrations – for example, the local gala day was held at nearby Govanhill Park.

There has, however, been a major change of fortunes in recent months. The HA has for some time been expanding into areas of wider action and has formed the Govanhill Community Development Trust. A community conference has identified the environment as a major source of concern. Funding has been obtained for GREAT (Govanhill Recycling and Environment Action Team), which is galvanising volunteers, schoolchildren and organisations (including the Larkfield Centre) in an energetic programme of gap-site,

recycling and gardening projects. It is possible that the maintenance of the space may be taken over by the association, and it certainly seems likely that the whole process will spawn community events in the space. In the meantime, the Millennium Hut – potting shed *extraordinaire* – is at last functioning in its intended use.

HAWTHORN

The client: Hawthorn Housing Co-operative Ltd

All community-based housing associations in Glasgow are small relative to national associations. The co-ops are smaller yet, and the Hawthorn Housing Co-op in Possilpark, north Glasgow, is one of these. It operates in a part of Possilpark that has been effectively razed to the ground. The co-op's developments stand amid green space laced with a street network now eerily devoid of houses, although re-building is slowly progressing. Physically, the area has none of the internal coherence of Govanhill; it also lacks Govanhill's presence in the spatial and perceptual map of Glasgow, being tucked away behind the area's main thoroughfare. That said, the co-op has a strong sense of itself, expressed in their strong engagement with the space project.

The brief: 'play on the edge'

Like Govanhill, Hawthorn had a well-developed idea of what it wanted. A former bowling green, now a derelict patch of grass with a diagonal desire line to the local shop, was identified as a site for play 'on the edge' and also as a visual focus for an area devoid of such landmarks. The long-term development plans were that the site would be surrounded on four sides by housing and perhaps a school, but the site is still open on two sides. The idea of *edgy play* derived from a piece of writing by another artist, insightfully commissioned independently by the co-op some time before. The real need in the area was for

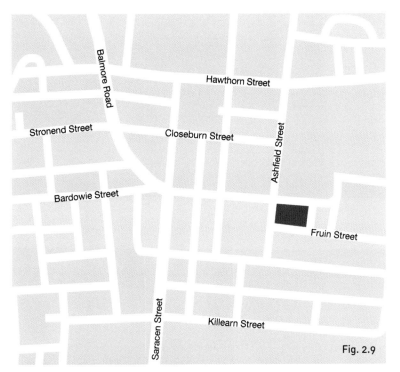

Fig. 2.9

Fig. 2.10

Fig. 2.12

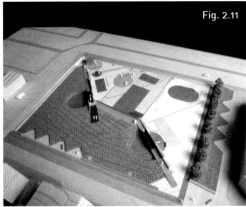

Fig. 2.11

Fig. 2.9. Hawthorn map

Fig. 2.10. Hawthorn: as with many others in the area, the site needed decontamination before work could begin

Fig. 2.11. Hawthorn: model, showing clearly the bays cut into the grassy raised area

Fig. 2.12. Hawthorn: dedicated graffiti wall with climbing walls and play bays just visible

engagement with the young people who normally hang out at swingparks; the idea was to give them their own space (the original conception incorporated a gallery of computers) and the little ones theirs. But it would have to be different – torching cars is a powerful alternative attraction.

The project

The co-op arguably set itself the tallest order of all the spaces, specifically looking for a place for play for a difficult age group. The clients were realistic about their user group and the designers went to great lengths to express these values in a place that also worked as a route and civic space for this small sub-area within Possilpark. Embracing the remit of toughness, the space is largely a field of inscribed concrete with occasional playful obstacles, and provides safe territory for young cyclists and games that require a hard surface (Fig. 2.13). The diagonal route was retained as the dividing line between the hard and soft elements, rising over a ramp supported by retaining gabion walls. Again, mounding was introduced to provide a green outlook to residents, and little bays were cut into this to create spaces for different types of play equipment (Fig. 2.14). The whole conception was formally quite unique and its unorthodox aesthetic was underlined by the artist's approach. While installing a set of colossal feet as a gesture to conventional ideas of public art (Fig. 2.15), he inscribed the concrete with grammar lessons, maps and first aid hints (Fig. 2.16). In the early days of the project, some genuinely witty pieces of graffiti from the local children affirmed the artist's conception.

The project was opened with much locally organised merrymaking on the day of the lunar eclipse, 1999 (Fig. 2.17).

Fig. 2.13

Fig. 2.14

Fig. 2.13. Hawthorn: ramps for cycles or skateboards

Fig. 2.14. Hawthorn: play 'bays' for younger children

Fig. 2.15. Hawthorn: 'Big Feet' sculpture (opening party)

Fig. 2.15

Fig. 2.16

Fig. 2.17

Fig. 2.16. Hawthorn: subliminal learning?—useful facts inscribed in concrete

Fig. 2.17. Hawthorn: opening party, designed and delivered by the housing co-op

The project revisited

Over the years, the project has slipped from tolerable hard wear to a position where it seems to have been rendered unattractive to the majority of users. The place *is* used, but it has been colonised by those young people whose behaviour alienates other users. There were unrealistic assumptions about the level of supervision and animation required to establish the space as safe and populated.

Fig. 2.18

Its primary provision, for play, is underused. Inevitably, a combination of factors contribute to this: design, vandalism, maintenance, supervision, vulnerability and local perception. The bays excavated from the grassy mounds are problematic because they cannot be monitored by CCTV cameras, and raise serious issues of maintenance and control for the future. All of the low-level lighting has long disappeared. The gabion baskets are being dismantled, despite the efforts of the co-op to mortar the rocks in place (Fig. 2.18). The local residents are vocal in their complaints, listing everything from people driving cars over dog-grills (or carrying their dogs over the same grills) to needles in the sandpit (Figs. 2.19–2.21).

Most significantly, the Land Services department stated that the space would *not* be adopted for full maintenance because of issues outstanding at the time of programmed handover. So the maintenance of this space, of all the most vulnerable, seems to reside in a no-man's land of basic council delivery and intermittent interventions by the housing co-op. This vitally important issue will be addressed in Chapter 3.

Fig. 2.18. Hawthorn: gabion walls destroyed, confirming local fears

Fig. 2.19. Hawthorn: play bays neglected and abused

Fig. 2.19

In spite of all of this, the space also provides the community with its own civic square. The co-op, pre-eminently among the 'space' associations and to its great credit, has struggled with the problems and has organised several events in the space (fireworks night, Halloween, fundraising galas). Furthermore, there have been efforts on the part of the co-op and individuals within it to address the question of underuse. Some of the older residents realised that children no longer seemed to know the street games that had been the common culture of Glaswegians for generations, so the co-op provided the props and a rota of local women took it in turn to go and play with the children, teaching them the games. This was very popular, and evolved into the Good Behaviour Club, all based on volunteer effort. Some younger women who came forward to help have taken up the challenge and, with the support of a community worker, are looking at play and social life for young people in the area. There is clearly great capacity and commitment here and with that comes hope that change may yet take place.

The co-op is faced with a complex situation. Here, the physical problems – part design-related, part maintenance, part active damage – have given the space a bad reputation. For a while it bore the damage well. With its tough aesthetic it was designed to absorb wear and tear, but too many hard knocks going beyond casual damage affect usability and drain the spirit. It has not been helped by the blight surrounding the site, which has if anything increased over the period. Indeed the local shop, a grim little shack but at least *there*, has now finally gone. Susan Brown, Director of the Hawthorn Housing Co-op put it well:

I think it is important to have someone who is responsible for the space afterwards. This is where the whole problem lies with our space.

The problem about bold endeavours in an area such as this is that they have to work, otherwise the resources of the neighbourhood – physical, financial, psychological and

Fig. 2.20

Fig. 2.20. Hawthorn: Big Feet – the remains

spiritual – are further stretched in attempting to sustain something that may have fundamental flaws. *Something happened* at Hawthorn, in 1999. People are living with the consequences. Justice demands that the imagination, modesty and cash be found to revisit the scene and finally deliver the vision.

Postscript: Summer 2004

It now seems possible that the council, majority owners of the land and to this extent responsible for safety, may make funds available for radical intervention, i.e. partial or wholesale clearance of the site. This would not be an unpopular move with many local people. The question is what happens afterwards. Perhaps the words of Susan Brown may point the way:

I think there may be another, more incremental way (to approach such projects). You start with a small space, designed as part of a larger space, but able to function independently. If this is successful, you add the other parts, piece by piece. If it is a failure, it is a small-scale failure.

Fig. 2.21

Fig. 2.21. Hawthorn: the 'shelter'

SARACEN CROSS

The client: Springburn and Possilpark Housing Association Ltd (SPHA)

Springburn and Possilpark were once famous the world over for the glories of their heavy engineering works: Springburn for its locomotives and Possilpark for its cast ironwork (a small example of which can be seen in the space as built). Hardly any trace remains of the massive presence of those industries. The HA has an office only a few hundred yards from that of the Hawthorn Co-op, reflecting the subtle territorial distinctions within the emergence of local housing provision. SPHA (now North Glasgow Housing Association) is the older, much bigger organisation (in Glasgow terms); the contrast in size and styles is part of the richness of the Glasgow movement.

The brief: an improved civic space

In contrast to Govanhill and Hawthorn, there was no strong programme from this housing association. The space at Saracen Cross consists of a triangular site created by a previous major realignment. The road is one of the main routes in the north of city and also what remains of the traditional tenemental main street of Possilpark. The space had been landscaped in a style common in the 1970s, with raised planting boxes and benches, but was overdue for reconsideration. The association pointed out that the first private sector housing for sale ever to be built in Possilpark faced on to the space, and that a quality environment would consolidate that investment and project a more positive image to further potential investors. (Projects of this type, in fact, can be seen as providing a generous subsidy to developers – something worth bearing in mind when the funding of future projects is considered. In some circumstances, instead of imposing an obligation to fund

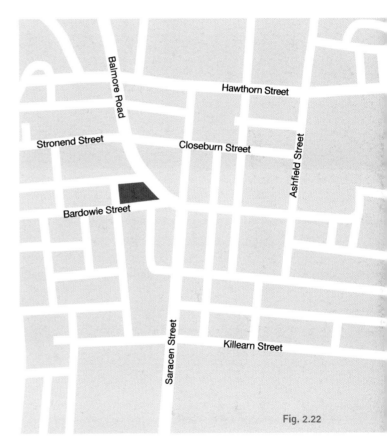

Fig. 2.22. Saracen Cross map

public space as part of a given development, might it be possible to provide the spaces and make a charge against developers? The local authority would thus be in charge of the strategic dimension of provision, not responding to a developer-led agenda.)

Fig. 2.23. Saracen: the site before

Fig. 2.25. Saracen: local children involved in planting

Fig. 2.24. Saracen: model

The project

The solution was an elegant and restrained programme of tree planting, granite paving and benches. The original collaboration between architect and artist foundered and was resolved in both contributions being largely independent of each other in delivery, although reading very successfully as an ensemble, as it turned out. The artist was very keen to evoke the *genius loci* and created, on the open edge of the site, a footprint of a typical tenement flat, looking at the past while anticipating the new development that would in due course occupy the site. In among this abstract patterning of dwarf walls and gravel, she planted a range of native perennials and shrubs (Fig. 2.25). The shrubs were contained in wire cages to protect them but also to allow them to be clipped into abstract shapes as they grew, thus creating an architectonic garden invaded by seemingly wild flowers.

Fig. 2.26. Saracen: on completion

The project revisited

This project has really survived quite well (Figs. 2.27–2.29). The inevitable graffiti is periodically removed (presumably by the council), and the trees and garden are flourishing. The cages around the shrubs have now been taken away but their geometric form has, to some extent, been respected. The HA did not take part in the review interviews, so it is not known by how much it has directly intervened. An important aspect of the artist's conception was the creation of a part-time gardener's post in collaboration with the HA and a training agency, and although this is now long past, it may have been sufficient to let the project literally take root. It was not a new space in the sense of the others – it would already have been part of the council's maintenance regime and it does not include any of the special features that the council warned against. It also benefits from its centrality and its position on one of the main routes through the north of the city. All of these may contribute to its relative success. In contrast to the Hawthorn space, it manages to send out a hopeful message for the wider area regeneration, which has still some way to go.

Fig. 2.27

Fig. 2.28

Fig. 2.27. Saracen: general view through site

Fig. 2.28. Saracen: a place for pause

Fig. 2.29. Saracen: the garden establishes itself

Fig. 2.29

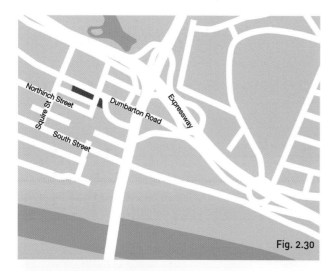

Fig. 2.30

Fig. 2.31

Fig. 2.30. Whiteinch Cross map
Fig. 2.31. Whiteinch: the site before

WHITEINCH CROSS

The client: Whiteinch and Scotstoun Housing Association Ltd (WSHA)

Another of the older associations, WSHA operates in the Dumbarton Road area, a canyon of tenements and infill that reaches for miles, from Yoker in towards Partick in the inner west end. Like Govanhill, it has a large stock of refurbished tenements, newbuilds and conversion. This association will soon move to multipurpose accommodation shared with local partners, again reflecting the established place of these organisations in the life of their areas.

The brief: Whiteinch Cross recreated

The long tenemental spine that was Dumbarton Road was ruptured in the 1960s by the creation of a slip road from the new Clyde Tunnel, just to the east of the chosen site. Demolition and low-rise re-building added to the incoherence. With the creation of newbuild housing on an important corner, the association aspired to create a focal point, a place recognisable as Whiteinch Cross by both local people and the many thousands who pass along this main artery into the city. The corner diagonally opposite the building and an adjacent open area, both with existing trees, seemed an ideal opportunity to provide this visual and civic focus and also to resolve the challenge of the tunnel exit.

The project

Although the space had a programme, for casual pause and encounter, its primary function was that of an urban marker, an emphatic stop to the vista along Dumbarton Road before the intrusion of the tunnel. In a skilful play of planes and materials, the designers created an abstract composition of vertical and horizontal surfaces. A 'waterwall' cascaded over Corten

Fig. 2.32

Fig. 2.33

Fig. 2.32. Whiteinch: model
Fig. 2.33. Whiteinch: the opening
ceremony...and much rain

Fig. 2.34

Fig. 2.35

(rusted) steel plate in evocation of the area's former shipyards. A giant white column emitted ultraviolet light, which grew in intensity as darkness fell. Wisteria was planted on a pergola. Landing lights were sunk into the ground among the trees (Figs. 2.34–2.36).

The project revisited

The ambition at Whiteinch was led by urban design imperatives, i.e. the need to distinguish the identity of the neighbourhood from its neighbours Partick and Scotstoun. The functional and civic dimensions of the project were whittled down by community feedback (a play area was rejected on safety grounds) or by budgetary constraints (which prohibited extending the project into the street and installing infrastructure for larger community events). Nevertheless, seating was an integral part of the scheme and was held to, despite negative feedback from some local residents. It was intended as a place to scan the newspaper on a sunny morning or for cyclists on the adjacent cycleway to have a sandwich. It was used for these purposes, although increasingly infrequently, as the sparkle wore off, and the water feature awaited major repair. Then an appalling blow was struck – destruction of the seating, requiring the application of

Fig. 2.34. Whiteinch: the water feature only functioned for a short time

Fig. 2.35. Whiteinch: the light column was meant to be a marker from a distance

Fig. 2.36

Fig. 2.36. Whiteinch: when newly complete, the night effect was stunning
Fig. 2.37. Whiteinch: one of many blows
Fig. 2.38. Whiteinch: Rusty Corten mysteriously 'tidied up'

Fig. 2.37

Fig. 2.38

considerable physical effort by local vandals (Fig. 2.37). A more institutional vandalism has seen the Corten steel painted battleship grey, though no doubt the shipbuilding reference this time was unintentional (Fig. 2.38). (Interestingly, no-one in the council can be found to admit to having done this, despite investigative efforts by the HA.) In spite of all this, the place is at least clean and tidy, but stripped of the many beautiful features that originally lit up this corner of the city. Perhaps the mixture of ingredients was simply too rich to be sustainable.

Whether the fortunes of the space were directly or indirectly influential, the fact is that in 2003 the local community forum appointed an environment officer, based at the HA, to implement a neighbourhood open-space strategy. The resulting Dumbarton Road Corridor Environment Trust should be well placed to combine strategic thinking and community engagement. The fear will be that the compromised outcomes of Whiteinch Cross will dull the appetite for truly special moments in the midst of more functional spaces. A delicate balance indeed.

GRAHAM SQUARE

The client: Molendinar Park Housing Association

Molendinar is in many ways untypical of the Glasgow housing associations, in being an offshoot (now fully independent) of Reidvale, one of the older community-based associations. This precocious youngster has a small stock, but has achieved eminence in Scotland and further afield[8] for the quality of its architecture, in particular the development at Graham Square, which is located around the public space of that name.

The brief: a leisure street

The unusual shape and character of Graham Square raised issues for the association as it embarked on the ambitious development of the site, using three of Scotland's foremost architectural practices in responding to the Grade A listed facades of the entrance to the former meat market. The site naturally divides into an inner and outer section. The concept of a *leisure street*, open to the public but not a thoroughfare, was hit upon for the outer space, with the inner one providing a more secluded retreat while still remaining technically public. A further constraint was that most of the houses surrounding the space would have no private space to the rear, implying a different relationship with the space in front. Another feature was the lack of an existing population; the very space that would be used most intensively by its public had no residents to be consulted at the time of designing.

The project

The strength of the built form, both old and new, required a lightness of touch in the creation of the spaces. What was delivered is, literally, a space, with the enigmatic calf sculpture ironically, tentatively, perched on his plinth, a lucky escapee

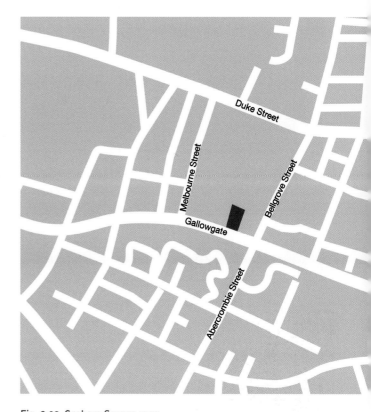

Fig. 2.39. Graham Square map

Fig. 2.40

from the past business of this place (Fig. 2.43). When photographed, this place seems to have the urbanity of a European piazza; in fact, it stands on the edge of an inner urban wasteland which the association now has a role in developing.

The inner garden is a picturesque foil to the hard outer court, somewhere perhaps to take a chair and a book, while a further small south-facing courtyard, exclusive to the residents of one block, can be tantalisingly glimpsed from this point (Fig. 2.44).

Fig. 2.41

Fig. 2.40. Molendinar: the site before
Fig. 2.41. Molendinar: model
Fig. 2.42. Molendinar: view of the completed outer courtyard

Fig. 2.42

The project revisited

The coherence of the whole project and its award-winning reputation has made Graham Square something of an icon of what affordable housing and good design are capable of. Despite unresolved issues with different council departments about maintenance (at least four separate council divisions have some stake in this), the association, which has its offices on the square, ensures that upkeep is of a standard befitting the project.

Fruit trees in the inner garden have now begun to produce healthy crops of apples and plums, a feature that is being repeated in Molendinar's next phase of development on an adjacent site. The overall configuration of an open yet well-defended formal courtyard progressing to individual gated housing blocks has been pursued in this development too.

As yet, the residents of Graham Square have not organised events in the space, but this is not the measure by which this project should be judged. Children play football in the outer court, their right to do so (until 9 pm) deliberated and established by the local management committee. And there will be time enough for events and rituals to evolve. We may yet perhaps see a harvest festival on the Gallowgate.

CONCLUSION

So there they are, five new little places for Glasgow, different in every respect apart from the circumstances of their delivery. They are different sorts of places, different in physical character and different in the interpretations put on them. The communities they serve are different and even their housing association champions responded to the challenge in different ways and with differing degrees of continuing commitment. In this respect they offer a rich source for reflection on a series of themes that are considered in the following chapters.

Fig. 2.44

Fig. 2.43

Fig. 2.43. Molendinar: the calf refers to the past life of the place

Fig. 2.44. Molendinar: the inner garden

Chapter 3

Case study issues and the policy context

INTRODUCTION

In 1996, when the Five Spaces project was conceived, the current interest in public space was hardly on the horizon. Certain seminal texts were published much earlier [2–5] or were beginning to create the discourse [6] but in the UK projects such as the Architecture Foundation's Creative Spaces [7] and Glasgow 1999's Five Spaces were some of the first to explore in ordinary neighbourhoods the themes being promulgated by advocates such as the Urban Design Group. Other policy concerns have brought the subject into increasingly sharp focus, to the point where, at the time of writing, public space is one of the key drivers of government policy.

WHY NOW?

A series of social phenomena and influential commentaries on them have converged to produce the current interest in public space (Figs. 3.1, 3.2). The discussion focuses on recognition of the following.

- Public space is *problematic*. Much of it is *badly designed*, *costly to maintain*, *underused*, and poses *threats to security*.

- Paradoxically, it is also a *public asset*; it is an important part of *urban heritage*, it makes a valuable contribution to *environmental quality*, *health and social cohesion*, and receives public endorsement as a *major contributor to quality of life*.

- It has unique status; *it defines us as citizens rather than as private individuals*.

- It is a *huge burden on the public budget* and a *challenge to physical and social planning*, encompassing everything from play provision to street design, civic space to football pitches and ranging in scale from Victorian parks to gap sites.

Fig. 3.1. Public space takes many forms: here, an uninviting (and dangerous?) portion of the Kelvin walkway, Glasgow. Walking is a central feature of sustainability and health agendas, raising issues of investment, management and design

Fig. 3.2. The joy that good space brings. Water is always an attraction, though expensive to manage and maintain. Here, exuberant occupation of the public realm (despite official deterrents). Parc André Citroën, Paris

- It is also increasingly seen as *expressing many of the symptoms of social exclusion.*
- It is the locus for a range of initiatives in *sustainable development.*
- It is looked to as a *potential driver of area regeneration.*

POLICY RESPONSES

Public space is therefore an area whose time has come. There are three drivers of UK policy:

- The concern for improved physical quality delivered by better design, integrated planning and partnership working.
- The understanding that common culture is expressed in this public domain; that it presents not only resources to be harnessed but also challenges for order and norms of behaviour.
- The understanding that some forms of social exclusion and their remedies may converge in engaging with the physical environment.

Both UK and Scottish policy-makers have developed a range of tools. Councils, other government agencies, the private and voluntary sectors are involved. More resources are certainly becoming available.

Undeniably, the Five Spaces project was a creature of a specific time, place and process. The issues that emerge from the individual project accounts are nevertheless entirely current. Some need immediate action on the ground, others provide graphic evidence of the complexity involved in turning a policy *fiat* into something that works on a number of important levels. Other aspects of the account may help to illustrate some of the less programmatic dimensions of public space provision, those elusive ingredients that can make or break a project.

This book does not examine the finer detail of the emerging policy landscape. Its focus is on the genesis and progress of a specific initiative and its conclusions are also action-orientated. Had the policy environment been hostile or indifferent, these proposals would hardly be worth making, since they assume a positive attitude, at the very least, to the experimental approach suggested.

The accounts below are taken from interviews with the HAs and consider all aspects of the project, from induction to maintenance. They expand on the issues raised in the project descriptions and the writer's comments are offered.

INDUCTION

The trip to Barcelona was spoken of with excitement and is invoked by participants in general discussions of design quality. The Art School event in particular was much praised. It was the energy and challenge of the event that remained with people as much as the specifics of the projects.

Comment

For a small investment relative to the amount expended on the project, the whole business of designing public space was put on the map for the HA clients whose involvement was such a central part of the project rationale. And not just for the chosen five – at that point 15 projects were envisaged. The exercise did not address itself to operational or embedded social issues; it was a brainstorming attack on a challenging proposition. Some of the relationships came to nothing; other consultants were brought on board. But neither was it entirely a 'blue sky' exercise, since from the start, the client was part of the debate.

We have suggested that it was the energising effect of the Barcelona and Art School experiences, rather than more measurable learning outcomes, that were their prime benefit.

It may be useful to consider whether more explicit lessons might also have been learned from the Barcelona trip, without compromising this broadening of view. For instance, had we visited a city with an urban culture more similar to that of Glasgow, would it have been possible to examine more closely the way in which young people are engaged or poor weather is dealt with? The unexamined transfer of practice from one to another very different context bedevils many projects that deserve much subtler thought. If designers are prey to this (which, of course, they should not be), clients should certainly be offered experiences that inspire but are also genuinely transferable, so that they, at least, are enabled to remain visionary *and* practical in their deliberations.

More careful consideration should be given to ways of creating ambition and exposure to new thinking. The old methods of community consultation are being replaced with more sophisticated tools, but there still remains the need to explore the issues, introduce possibilities and innovative thought without simply bewitching people with seductive imagery. *But enchantment is legitimate and necessary.* A structured and supported debriefing session, properly recorded, might help to achieve this delicate balance.

PROJECT RELATIONSHIPS

The most strongly made observation was that associations are experienced project managers with multimillion pound budgets and long experience in the field of area regeneration, and so would have been entirely capable of running their own scheme and exercising tighter client control. The original intention was exactly this, but the demands of the 1999 programme dictated a more centralised approach. Asked in the interview whether there would be an outright objection to project delivery across sites in the future, the associations remained open-minded but insisted on individual control over specification and quality. It remains to be seen whether the

two might be compatible: economies of scale and programming along with the local control expected by the associations.

There are several points in the responses where associations felt that their stipulations over significant elements of design had been over-ruled or compromised in some way. These range from fundamental concerns (e.g. the 'bays' in the Hawthorn scheme being out of sight and therefore difficult to supervise) to matters of detail, in which the designers, too, (though this is anecdotal) felt less in control over changes than they might have done. This meant that details that turned out to be critical were changed, e.g. the size and gauge of the mesh used in the gabion baskets at Hawthorn and the disposition of savings at Whiteinch across the site instead of the available funds being concentrated in one area.

Comment

The first point to be emphasised is that the associations understood the motivations and circumstances that produced the project relationships that emerged. They took an opportunity offered to them, and if they would have preferred greater control over the running of the schemes, they understood the constraints. Nevertheless, their comments are important in two ways: first, in distinguishing avoidable shortcomings of design and fabrication from issues of maintenance and use; second, in the context of future best practice in the commissioning and direction of such developments.

The narrative also illustrates how every stage in the process of realising public projects is subject to the whim of external and internal circumstance. The Five Spaces project is unusual in being both high profile (and major in terms of public strategy and investment) and sufficiently small for the relationship of individual actors and circumstances in the process to be described and learnt from.

COMMUNITY INVOLVEMENT AND EDUCATION

If community involvement is second nature to the associations' view of themselves, the mediation of a project such as Five Spaces presented new challenges. To whom exactly did the project address itself? How could quite bold design ideas be communicated to an audience new to the very concept of 'public space'? How could the role of inspired client be reconciled with community responsiveness?

The funders, particularly the Scottish Arts Council, insisted that education and marketing should be integral to the project; indeed, it was a condition of funding.

Local communication

Each association was asked to produce a consultation plan appropriate to local circumstances.

- *Whiteinch* held library exhibitions and meetings and made use of the local newspaper. The association was satisfied with the degree of local feedback, and felt the project and its rationale had been adequately communicated.

- *Govanhill,* too, held an open evening and also had the benefit of the artist's residency to establish local relationships. However, the representatives felt that this aspect should receive more attention in similar situations in future. The situation was further complicated by the presence on the site of a local community education centre that was identified as having a special relationship to the creation of activity within the space; however, this was an informal understanding that seems not to have borne fruit to date.

- *Springburn and Possilpark* had the advantage of an office overlooking their space at Sacaren Cross, so had a display and open session in addition to coverage in the local paper.

- *Hawthorn*, a very much smaller neighbourhood, had a particular constituency to reach – its young people. The architects took an imaginative route into this. Understanding that their user group would not turn up to a standard meeting, they took a projector out into the space on a winter evening and showed computer simulations of the project (Fig. 3.3). This was, admittedly, carried out at an early stage, and the scheme was not delivered until over two years later. The interviews demonstrate that some people now involved with the co-op did not recall being consulted, but as a fellow interviewee wryly remarked, it is the co-op's experience that it is almost impossible to avoid such charges, despite exhaustive attempts to communicate the issue of the day. Opinion after the fact is always much more readily obtainable. Notwithstanding this, there is a clear need to reach people in ways that provoke response, or at least tacit assimilation of what is going on, and to maintain that contact.

- In *Molendinar Park's* case, the semi-private nature of the space and the fact that there was no resident community made communication less of a priority. The scheme had already attracted press attention in the city for the artwork proposal by Kenny Hunter for a golden calf atop a column (which was modified after debate within the management committee).

Fig. 3.3. Hawthorn: images shown in the open air attempted to engage young people

Fig. 3.3

Education

The education dimension was developed by the Glasgow 1999 Education Team, who devised sessions in local schools on designing open spaces. In some cases, management committee members went into classrooms to recount their memories of how the neighbourhood had changed. This was very successful but, again, could have been further developed and, indeed, similar work is now being carried out by the Lighthouse education and community teams[9].

Comment

As events have shown, attempts at communicating the projects were inadequate in some cases. What would have succeeded? Clearly the communication of a space presented a different challenge from a presentation about the next new housing project. Was it the designs that were wrong, or the way they were introduced to local people? Might a greater degree of hands-on involvement in their conception and making have contributed to greater success? If the spaces had been better managed (discussed further below) might they have eventually endeared themselves, once the shock of the new had passed?

The possibility is that, for the majority of residents, and in spite of the consultation and the enthusiasm of their sponsoring housing association, the spaces were construed as a top-down initiative, welcome inasmuch as something was being done in the area but, to many, alien in their aesthetics and rationale[10].

MAINTENANCE

Association representatives unanimously stated that there was no clear understanding of the maintenance regime undertaken and delivered by the City Council. This lack of baseline awareness made all other observations on upkeep somewhat provisional, since there was no clarity as to whether specific problems were one-off omissions or simply not provided for at all.

Comment

The issue of maintenance was seen as crucial from the start. Funders insisted on formal undertakings, and the City Council Land Services department was involved in scrutinising the plans with a view to making this commitment. Indeed there were several issues on which the council took a firm view, not least the health and safety standards at the Hawthorn playground. There were observations of a more general nature with regard to design, but generally the department embraced the ethos of the project. On one issue, however, there was some substantial difficulty – the so-called 'special features', ranging from the waterwall at Whiteinch (water features are a perennial headache for parks departments) to the care of more conventional artworks such as Molendinar's calf or Hawthorn's Big Feet sculptures.

The council always stated that the maintenance and possibly even replacement of such features lay beyond the scope of its budgets, which have been progressively squeezed over recent years. The only other long-term parties in the project were the housing associations, so there was the suggestion that they should assume some responsibility. This proposal was never formally presented to the associations, still less accepted, since the associations had neither ownership of the land nor funds other than rental income to sustain such expenditure. Individual associations, however, have made a range of informal interventions, some one-off, some regular, to mitigate what they see as the deterioration of their space. Examples are Whiteinch's contract with the Westworks community enterprise to litter-pick, power-hose and remove graffiti, and Hawthorn's modifications to the dog-grills.

SECURITY

There were some strong comments from Hawthorn relating to the spatial arrangements that enabled people to remain unseen in the play bays carved out of the mounded areas. CCTV cameras were unable to survey these areas, which contain play equipment behind a sandpit. All these areas have been compromised by discarded needles, bottles and other evidence of negative behaviour (such as the partial dismantling of the brickwork retaining the bridge structure). Lighting of these areas is inadequate, so that people using the diagonal route through the space, itself well lit, are unsure of who else is in there.

Generally, replacement of light fittings was a problem, both aesthetically and in terms of security. A large and vulnerable part of the Hawthorn space was also in darkness on an evening visit in autumn. The bulbs of the landing lights in the grassed area at Whiteinch have not been replaced since they failed; at the last visit there were no lights at all in the whole space. Ground lights/bulkhead lights were almost universally destroyed in all the spaces within months of their being installed, and these have not been replaced. (They are extremely vulnerable, and this should be a watchpoint for any future schemes.) Without light the space is less safe.

In addition to the actual risks posed by inadequately lit or overlooked spaces, the sight of vandalised and poorly used spaces contributes to a sense of perceived insecurity/risk, particularly important if parents are to feel confident about their children using such spaces.

Comment

The problem of lighting (specification, replacement and general maintenance) is not peculiar to Glasgow. Paradoxically it is one of the elements of urban furnishing that can act most potently – for good or ill – in a number of practical and aesthetic ways. The value of this is recognised by Glasgow City Council in its new lighting strategy [8] and in *2020 Vision* [9], a document that reported an average repair turnaround of three days. The Five Spaces project clearly represented a non-standard solution and one in which this department did not have a lead role. There are no doubt issues arising from this situation that might be eliminated in future projects. As the visual and amenity value of lighting is recognised in the design of spaces, rather than operating as a separate and purely functional element of municipal provision, the operational demands of this will increase. Furthermore, as the lighting strategy takes hold, refinements are to be expected. But the basic challenge remains – to ensure the lights stay on.

IMAGE

Opinions on this issue range from one extreme to the other. Molendinar's ensemble piece at Graham Square has set the standard for inner city living, turning a derelict fragment into a catalyst of change in a wider area. The benefits of this are not lost on the new residents, whose houses are visited by regeneration tourists from far and wide. More important, self-esteem and pride in the development are clearly in evidence, from the proliferation of potted plants in the sunspaces to the more worldly indicator of rising house prices. The space has yet to be assigned an explicit role in the life of the new community, but its quiet quality even now acts as an elegant container for that emerging life.

Despite some problems, Govanhill's space is deemed to have enhanced the image of the area, and although there is work to be done to develop its full potential for conviviality, the signs are most hopeful. There is a much greater degree of ambivalence, however, on the part of Hawthorn and Whiteinch. Even allowing for the anecdotal nature of some of the verdicts, it is clear that, taking everything into account, the projects are seen as problematic to the identity of the neighbourhood, both to outsiders and to the perception of the area by the people who live there.

Associations remained glad to have created the spaces, but were uncertain about the degree of local acceptance. Evidence taken on the streets supports this confusion. Many were glad to see the interventions as a sign of something being done, but less enthusiastic about the use or aesthetics of the projects.

THE ROLE OF PUBLIC SPACE IN THE HOUSING ASSOCIATIONS' OUTLOOK

In asking questions about use, the idea was to get beyond operational matters. Had the original brief set a strong direction for the project? To what extent was it true to speak of an evolving culture, a set of uses and meanings, which in turn might contribute to the overall life of the neighbourhood?

All the associations said that public space was important to them, but that funding and programming made it difficult to make integrated plans. Most had found the experience of involvement in the Five Spaces project instructive, although, significantly, Whiteinch felt that committee enthusiasm for another such project would be in question after negative feedback about their space. Govanhill saw the need for a vision, which should then be tested in a high-quality consultative process. However, the dense layout of their area, determined by the tenemental form, precluded any radical interventions; it now remained more a matter of responding to the potential of small gap sites. It was mentioned that the association was thinking about an overall environmental strategy, which of course is now in place. They were insistent on the need for ambitious design: 'people don't think good design is important until they get it' (Robert Farrell, committee member). Hawthorn felt the issue was of vital significance.

FUTURE PROJECTS?

Associations' enthusiasm for new endeavours was less evident than their commitment to their existing spaces. Comments were offered on the advisability of starting with smaller projects, working upwards in scale from community gardens with lots of hands-on involvement, temporary projects towards the more ambitious, more civic projects such as the Five Spaces. Control over access was also seen to be a significant element.

Would associations wish to design and manage space, and how did this relate to owning it?

- *Whiteinch* said the council should deliver and maintain, unless *real* ownership could pass to the association.
- *Molendinar* felt associations did not do enough of this kind of work to build up a body of expertise. Should a city-wide dedicated group including association committee members learn about the issues and share the experience?
- *Govanhill* was of the view that, subject to funding, the Govanhill Community Development Trust would take on this type of project.
- *Hawthorn* felt it was a job for the council, with thorough local co-operation and involvement.

OWNERSHIP

Ownership is a term with wide currency in community development circles. It carries a useful ambivalence, referring at once to physical, even legal possession, but also to an emotional or cultural investment in an idea or an object that may be additional to, or independent of, legal claim. Thus the housing association clients were seen as having ownership of the design process with its attendant responsibility of ensuring local participation. They were also entrusted with what we might call *cultural* ownership. Having been central to the creation and communication of the scheme, the task of continuing to uphold the project in this non-material way has naturally fallen to them. The Glasgow 1999 Company led the overall project, under licence from the City Council, and so had ownership of the delivery on the ground. Its Land Services department has continuing ownership of the maintenance regime, while various council departments have legal ownership of almost all of the land.

Described in this way, the chain of ownership is seen to have some weak links. The associations have a range of strong opinions on issues such as maintenance and the animation of the spaces. They feel responsible for the project, but have no actual authority or resources to act. To be sure, there is nothing to prevent them from organising activities or making their space a focus of local environmental initiatives. But the emotional ownership isn't there.

There is also the issue of much wider local ownership, that intangible quality which manifests itself in positive use, growing affection, and eventually perhaps its own micro-culture and rituals. The whole ethos of participation, rooted in the housing associations, is intended to deliver this feeling of *ours* as opposed to *no-one's*.

But this is not housing. These sites are parts of the totality of public spaces throughout the city, part of a spectrum that ranges from Victorian parks to riverbanks to pedestrian precincts. As such they are properly the business of the council, the strategic authority charged with developing the public culture of the city. They are also the concern of the people of Glasgow as a whole, in whose name the council is charged with city beautification and management. These particular spaces are however poised on that knife-edge between local and civic ownership, where local understanding, local knowledge is in the 'ownership' of local people, who may be the key resource to ensure the effective operation of that place, to give it life, and to avoid endless expenditure on the remediation of vandalism and negative use.

There is also the more pressing issue of hard cash, which relates in a direct way to the cultural ownership theme. Who controls the way in which these spaces are run – and that means who holds the purse strings – is clearly important to the feeling of empowerment and responsiveness. Legal ownership of the sites may be inconsequential; it is ownership of what happens above ground and the means to deliver that are crucial.

So perhaps is it is unrealistic to distinguish this real ownership, with clear, resourced responsibility, from the symbolic ownership described above. New arrangements are needed to relocate critical functions within the areas themselves. The growth of community gardens, city farms and playparks initiated, developed and managed by local groups demonstrates what real 'ownership' can deliver.

THE PRESSING ISSUES

Operational issues

It is difficult to exaggerate the importance of maintenance in these spaces. If it is important to keep the streets clean, it is doubly important to demonstrate that these special spaces are being cherished, to build up the ownership, the credibility of the space. The Five Spaces did not fit easily into the council's palette of open spaces – that was clear from the start. As a result they have fared badly under its maintenance regime. Failures of communication between the various parties throughout the process resulted in a stalemate where no-one had clear responsibility and the spaces looked likely to degrade progressively. Where this has not yet been done, there is a clear and urgent need to establish the following.

■ What exactly the council has specified by way of cleaning, maintenance of soft and hard landscaping, routine replacement of fittings (e.g. lights), servicing and repair of mechanical features, and at what frequencies.

- How the council sees its role with regard to the question of malicious damage, both in terms of general policy and cash resources.
- The other areas in which the council is unable to service the space, either in terms of cost or other factors.
- A provisional strategy for managing deficiencies in the short term until a more coherent system is agreed.

Remediation

The spaces were expensive and it is important that that investment is not lost. In the cases of Whiteinch and Hawthorn, consideration needs to be given to remediation works; for Hawthorn, a programme of support and activity development is required. It is unclear who will take the lead on this. The HAs are the obvious agencies, and it is to be hoped that they will do so. But the negative reactions to the spaces experienced by the associations are unlikely to predispose them to positive intervention; damage limitation seems to be more the attitude.

CONCLUSION

Writing this part of the book was not the most cheering of experiences. However, there is the danger of missing the point. In looking again at the Five Spaces, we can detect, underneath the crucial and undeniable management issues, a range of important themes that can help inform the development of neighbourhoods. The emergence of a range of policy initiatives, critical thought and practical experiments suggests that the time may be right to devise ways of realising their potential.

Chapter 4

Special places: 'civic' space in the neighbourhood

INTRODUCTION

This book grew out of an ambition informed by quite practical impulses – to look at a project and explore the issues around it. Some of the issues raised by the Five Spaces are specific to the project's time, place and mode of delivery. But the project also has dimensions that are of quite telling currency.

New policy, especially that of sustainable development, offers a possible synthesis of physical and social imperatives. If the mechanisms are still unfolding, the general direction is sound. However, despite the current emphasis on public realm issues, a lack of policy attention to the kind of local *civic* space typified by the Five Spaces reveals a more general lack of clarity about the importance of the public domain in non-central locations. These deeper considerations argue for a much more subtle interrogation of the nature of place; of the cultural as well as physical challenges of creating and maintaining them.

GREEN VERSUS GREY

Green space has always been an important feature of the urban landscape but it was overdue for a re-appraisal. Its significance for health and wellbeing, visual amenity and citizenship has been re-asserted and reflected in a series of influential reports, and is now enshrined in government policy [10, 11]. What is less clear is the nature of civic (also referred to as *grey* or *hard*) space[11], for what is the '*civis*' in the contemporary world? Is urbanity to be measured in the number of designer stores attracted to our carefully streetscaped pedestrian zones? Policies of course mention civic space, but specific comment tends to be confined to city centre projects. It seems then that we need a view of what contemporary urbanity might be about. Without at least an ambition to understand this, each new endeavour is liable to be one more technical fix in the urban landscape.

The great green spaces of the 19th century were parks, built as the lungs of industrial cities (Fig. 4.1). Their civic spaces were its squares (many of them of earlier date), crossroads and markets, churchyards and memorials (Figs. 4.2, 4.3). Provided or improved by private capital or municipal zeal, they were the stage-set for social life, understood and used by most members of society for trade, exchange, socialising and ceremony. City improvements enshrined this reality, monumentalising victories, benefactors and heroes of all kinds (Fig. 4.4).

While this was going on, an intellectual and spiritual revolution was occurring. Crises of faith, political upheaval, cultural fragmentation, technological progress – the birth of modernism – situated the individual in a very different relationship to these outer worlds. The city began to be intelligible only in the gathered fragments of subjective experience. The world of pageant, religious and political ritual began to fall away into anachronism, leaving only the hectic, rich, endlessly changing texture of urban life. The person on the Clapham omnibus looks out on the world, then steps off and is lost in the crowd. Modernity, the experience of the 20th century, is about this poise between being known (in some kind of community) and being anonymous (and therefore free to become) (Fig. 4.5). It is the predicament of urban man, considered by writers from Jane Jacobs [5] to Richard Sennet [12]. Such insights help explain the problematic status of the public realm, while simultaneously upholding its indispensability to what we recognise as *city*.

PRIVATE AND PUBLIC

The public realm experienced by many today is as likely as not to be privately owned: shopping malls, leisure complexes, private gardens (Fig. 4.6). Popular and convenient as these places may be, they pose a challenge to the concept of public space – they are not public. The public is admitted, usually so

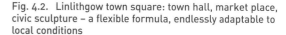

Fig. 4.2. Linlithgow town square: town hall, market place, civic sculpture – a flexible formula, endlessly adaptable to local conditions

Fig. 4.1

Fig. 4.2

Fig. 4.5

Fig. 4.3

Fig. 4.4

Fig. 4.1. Tollcross Park, in Glasgow's east end: an industrialist's mansion and estate acquired by the city for the health and leisure of working people. The house was for many years the city children's museum

Fig. 4.3. Parkhead Cross, Glasgow: once the hub of shopping and services in the east end, now a congested crossroads drained of life by the adjacent Forge (shown in Fig. 4.6)

Fig. 4.4. Cathedral Square, Glasgow: Monument to John Arthur, 'a memorial of respect and esteem from those who were in his employment'

Fig. 4.5. Buchanan Street: Glasgow's showcase walking street and its retail hub

they may spend money, but these spaces are not *city*. The truly public realm is therefore forced to contend with at least two realities:

- the fall of 'public man' – the decline of an individual's ability to locate her or himself within a commonly shared set of assumptions and norms as to how to behave in and relate to the city
- the rise of private 'public' space (and private leisure).

Despite the brevity of this account, it signals a level of thinking about the city that we ignore at our peril. It is impossible to create value-free spaces according to some urban design formula or in evocation of a civic golden age. All interventions are informed by a set of latent or explicit assumptions and

drivers, and it is important that as far as possible these should be clearly understood. The best public spaces are those that can expand from their original intention, accommodating new uses and conditions, constantly enriching their stock of meanings and associations. In the literal sense, they are the repository of a city's life. Public spaces require a cultural argument, but one that is neither too explicit or literal, leaving space for this accrual of meaning. A space should be full, but not 'full up'.

Fig. 4.6. Forge shopping mall, Parkhead, Glasgow: private 'public' space draws life away from the streets

Fig. 4.6

CIVIC SPACE IN NEIGHBOURHOODS

The historic city cores can probably continue to carry these changes of meaning and use without losing the deeper resonances described above. George Square, Glasgow's main civic space, still manages to hang on to its gravitas, and has hosted Nelson Mandela as well as the Christmas ice rink. Walter Scott and Robert Burns look down from their plinths on anti-war demonstrations and Remembrance Day events (Figs. 4.7, 4.8). But out in the neighbourhoods, urbanity is forgotten. Neither garden suburb nor urban district, the newer estates do their best with front gardens and 'amenity space'. Closer into the city, the fragmentation persists (with few exceptions) despite massive investment and considerable achievement in housing regeneration (Fig. 4.9).

Perhaps there is no need for a civic realm in these neighbourhoods. Perhaps contemporary civic life is so diminished that this should be admitted, and effort concentrated on pretty gardens and health and fitness spaces, with the parks accommodating the occasional rally or

Fig. 4.7. George Square, Glasgow: demonstrations in front of the City Chambers are a cherished part of political culture. The location is important, resonating with echoes of previous struggles

Fig. 4.7

Fig. 4.8

Fig. 4.9

Fig. 4.8. George Square, Glasgow: the winter festival sees the square transformed with ice rink and funfair

Fig. 4.9. Gallowgate, Glasgow: city, suburb or urban neighbourhood? This 1970s inner city development is currently the subject of a highly innovative collaboration (part of the National Programme for Architecture), embracing many of the themes raised in this book; many others are not so lucky

tree-planting ceremony. More significantly, did these places ever have a civic realm? Was public space not always the preserve of the city centre? This is true to a large extent, but Glasgow's urban landscape of the early 20th century produced a public realm as rich as any of Jane Jacobs' New York scenarios: streets of tenements, consistently strong in their form, whether modest or more pretentious in detail; fine architecture around the crosses, embellished by the occasional fountain, drinking well, monument, even bandstand. By these means one place was able to distinguish itself from another within a common urban framework, providing an intense environment for daily exchange and communal ritual. Today, such fragments as have survived serve more as urban reproach than urban resource (Fig. 4.3).

Fig. 4.10

Fig. 4.10. City of London: amid the bustle of contemporary life, a flashback to more basic concerns, the provision of unpolluted drinking water for citizens

A PLACE FOR RITUAL

Perhaps these daily encounters now take place in the supermarket, a car journey away, but the difference is that they occur in a specialised environment rather than in the context of a space that is also the way home, the path to school or the post office: a *place* in other words.

Nostalgia is dangerous. Too busy with the past, it ignores the potential of our own time. The question is this: amid the commodification of the urban experience expressed in the shopping mall, the heritage ride, the leisure industry, is there still potential in the forming of neighbourhoods for little spaces of contradiction, which stand aside from the transience of the here and now and testify to the past of a place and its future possibility (Fig. 4.10)?

A dangerous thought, for if there is in fact no such need, such places are not simply expensive and irrelevant, they are a burden for those on whom they are visited. What must be present – and what the historic city may have had – is a sense of the fittingness of such developments, when people would pay by public subscription for the erection of a monument [13].

THE ROLE OF PUBLIC ART

At a time when shared cultural and religious belief cannot be assumed (and diversity and plurality are to be welcomed) we see people finding other routes into human solidarity, the most telling being the outpouring of sentiment at the scenes of accidents or murders or at proxy locations. An example is the creation of a virtual shrine at Kenny Hunter's Citizen Fire-fighter in the aftermath of September 11, 2001 (Fig. 4.11). Clearly there is a deep-felt need not just to unite in spirit but to make a mark across boundaries of geography and culture.

Citizen Fire-fighter is an interesting character. He is a type (brave public servant) but he also challenges the stereotype (of heroic worker). He is anonymous, rather short and clumsy-looking under his protective gear – slightly sinister even. Neither monumentalised martyr nor idealised servant, he testifies to the difficulty of defining and portraying heroes, even the few (such as fire-fighters) who have survived the cynicism of the modern age. By subverting the tradition of municipal statuary, Hunter is able to make figurative works that speak powerfully to the modern audience.

In referring to Citizen Fire-fighter and to the need to memorialise, the contentious topic of public art comes into view. Despite the dismal failure of much public art of recent decades, it is in the enquiries of artists (and artists' collaborations) rather than architectural programmes that some of the most penetrating attempts to understand the nature of public space can be found. But much of this is conceptual, embedded in the thinking rather than part of the built reality. Faced with the difficulties of the Five Spaces projects and the many theoretical issues that beset the emergence of an adequate point of view, faintheartedness about the public art route is forgivable but regrettable.

TOWARDS RICHER PLACES

It has been argued that attempts at civic scale are highly desirable and indeed crucial, in the context of urban renewal areas, where strength in urban form and individual buildings is often lacking and where the creation of local identity asks for more than a playpark or even green space. However, we contend, such initiatives are at one end of a spectrum of spatial interventions. At the opposite extreme lie much more modest exercises in engagement, whether physical or more broadly cultural. Spaces of civic ambition should only be created where there is demonstrable, genuine engagement and consent from local people (Fig. 4.12). Where this can be demonstrated, the ambition and its challenges must be

Fig. 4.11. Glasgow: Citizen Fire-fighter became a spontaneous shrine after September 11

Fig. 4.11

developed and held to, not dissipated in some homogenised prettification. It does not mean that people have to make the spaces themselves, nor even have to maintain them (although this might be a useful outcome).

Where the circumstances are right for their creation, civic space in neighbourhoods must be of the *highest quality*. If it is important to grace the city centre with open space worthy of its fine buildings, the role of design in the non-central locations is arguably even more important to people's lives, redeeming the fractures of past redevelopment or the mediocre generality of the built fabric. The ambitions of Govanhill and Whiteinch for gateways or markers to their areas, for instance, spoke of a real thirst for local identity.

Local appropriateness is also crucial. We have seen the importance of getting the project right, both as to general orientation ('What do we really need here?') to fine-tuning the details of project design ('We want the delight of ground lights without the grief they cause'). If the precept is true for houses or health centres, it is arguably more so in this case, where the user/client base is indeterminate and fickle. People are obliged to use buildings about which they may have reservations; but they avoid spaces they deem worthless.

Both these values, *design quality* and *appropriateness*, are non-negotiable. One of the abiding challenges for those interested in quality urban regeneration is to foster an interest in bold and creative design while remaining true to the ethos of real responsiveness. If the two cannot be held in creative tension, there are two possible approaches. The first is of manageable mediocrity, something that can be kept clean and tidy but isn't worth a second look. The other is of the controversial intervention that never earns its place in the life of the neighbourhood, and declines into disuse and dereliction. Faced with those extreme alternatives, it is easy to see why the clean and tidy option is the choice most authorities make.

Fig. 4.12

Fig. 4.12. Nou Barris, Barcelona. A local struggle to 'win' a civic space for the neighbourhood is celebrated in the sculpture, Republica. Claiming the streets has strong resonances for Spaniards

In studying this area of work at close range, there is the danger of seeing every roadside verge and playpark as needing to be charged with physical and cultural significance. This of course is practical and theoretical nonsense; the council can't create such gems and citizens would very soon tire of such a rich diet. Rather, the requirement for most of us is that incidental spaces should be clean, tidy, pleasing, safe and well integrated with the built form of the city. Glasgow has many thousands of pieces of such land in its total portfolio and carries the burden of measuring up to that challenge.

The Five Spaces project didn't merely set out to produce another five for that list. They were quite clearly meant to be different. In city strategic terms, they require the embracing of a category of *local civic space*, along with a general reassertion of the values of urbanity. After all, a place may only need good streets, not a drinking fountain, to create the resonance (or capacity for it) we have described. Local civic space should be embraced as a principle, with suitable design and civic ambition, but these special places (such as the Five Spaces) should only be progressed when there is sufficient local cultural weight behind such an intervention to render the thing credible, and, in fact, needed.

NEIGHBOURHOOD CIVIC SPACE: A CHECKLIST

A new awareness of sense of place is abroad, from policy through to individual local initiatives of all kinds. A sense of the physical environment as the setting for lives as well for commerce; a straining away from monoculture towards celebration of tradition and diversity; confronting the challenges of global versus local, centralism versus devolution: it's a good time to be engaged in this work.

There is the danger, though, that the manifest difficulties of the Five Spaces programme preclude further experiments in this high-risk terrain. This would be regrettable. These attempts at civic scale are crucial in the context of urban renewal areas. It is in these areas that strength in urban form and individual buildings is often lacking, and where the creation of local identity asks for more than a playpark or even green space.

Within this new typology of neighbourhood space, civic space might be expected to have some of the following features.

- It would probably be hard, or mostly so.
- It would provide a focal point or punctuation mark in the local scene.
- It would have a self-evident programme for active and/or passive use, but would not require an elaborate narrative.
- It would be distinctive; providing identity, both for inhabitants and to those from outside.
- It would be locally significant, commemorating or celebrating.
- It would simply be beautiful for its own sake – a highly designed urban object, e.g. a lighting installation (such as Cranhill Water Tower, see later) or a fountain.
- It would be maintained to the highest specification – a standard bearer for the area.
- It would be linked, both visually and physically, with the rest of the area.
- It would be subject to passive surveillance from surrounding buildings.
- It would be animated in ways appropriate to its character.

This list combines elements of urban design, cultural significance, urban management and even place-marketing for regenerated neighbourhoods. In this respect it is exemplary of the type of integrative thinking in which we are being encouraged.

The risk is that the more superficial aspects of such space-making are easily delivered, while underlying issues are neglected. The crucial dimension is that such space is meaningful, holding sufficient worth and significance for enough people to enable it to root in local culture. Good existing examples of this category are hard to find. It may be that the total number of these special places turns out to be very limited (therefore enhancing their special status), and that resources are better deployed in more modest interventions. But that all remains to be explored.

A CHALLENGE TOO FAR?

Civic space – the very words suggest the responsibility of the city as opposed to individual communities of interest or neighbourhoods. Attempts to deliver such projects are fraught with difficulty, inviting one or more of the following conclusions.

■ They are no longer culturally tenable (people have moved to indoor space and other more private diversions). The city centre looks as if it will be the sole preserve capable of holding these meanings.

■ They have to be delivered from the grassroots, and possibly maintained by them. They are thus highly 'owned' but have limitations as to design and specification and therefore are not suitable for every situation.

■ The city is indeed responsible for making and maintaining these spaces, implying a strategic and resource commitment. A high degree of community involvement is taken as read, but the abiding problems of top-down initiatives are still present. And is the same approach appropriate both to a playpark and to the creation of civic space?

■ There is a basic conflict between the demands of project development/delivery in these areas and the capturing of some sense of *genius loci*. No matter if we employ all the participatory tools and the best designers, there is still

something in the culture that fundamentally challenges this idea of local civic space.

Even if such pessimistic perspectives are rejected, it has to be admitted that the agenda is tough:

■ to create civic space in regeneration settings where there is none or very little of it on the ground

■ to deliver community involvement, without which there is disaster

■ to produce designs that offer something to the wider fabric of the city rather than simply providing a neighbourhood amenity

■ to stimulate and respond to a part of our nature as citizens, that part which is precisely not that of today and its needs, but locates us in relation to the past and future

■ to deliver such spaces in a way that supports rather than contradicts wider moves towards sustainable development on physical, social and economic fronts, while admitting the possibility that such spaces may be more technically complex than the more participatory approach appropriate to other kinds of spaces.

CONCLUSION

This chapter has asserted the value of a particular type of public space: that is the civic, ceremonial, symbolic episodes that help to bring identity and focus into ordinary urban neighbourhoods. It has been useful to concentrate on the features of this type of space since, to the extent that we have defined a typology, the Five Spaces fall into this category.

In that process, however, a new wider landscape of concerns has opened up, which is even more confusing and complex. In the process comes the growing conviction that it will be in the messy, ordinary spaces of neighbourhoods that a place's life will be found.

Chapter 5

Common places: the public space of neighbourhoods

INTRODUCTION

This chapter extends the speculation outwards from the consideration of special projects such as the Five Spaces into the general territory of neighbourhood space. The suggestion will be that, counter-intuitive though it may be for designers, we have to reverse the primacy of physical design in favour of what might be called *culture* – the way people live. That is what design is about, surely, and there is certainly no thought here to consign designers once again to the land of paving and plantboxes, to a reactive role that falls back on some bland 'participatory' precept. Common place is no place for bravura statement or facile convention. It needs less *and* more.

THE WORLD OF COMMON PLACE

Beginning with the jarring experience of a toe stubbed on a broken pavement, through the operational issues raised in road mending, back to the subjective apprehension of belonging, all the way through the designer's attempts to synthesise physical programme and symbolic value, and beyond, to structural and even metaphysical speculation, it looks like public space in this sense defies the single view. It is almost too big to deal with, certainly for those who aspire to apply the insights of analytical thought to the creation of real spaces in real time.

So what can be agreed? Louis Kahn's dictum 'The street is a room by agreement... its ceiling is the sky' [see 14] seems inclusive enough. The single defining quality of the public realm is that *it belongs to everyone and to no-one*. Of course physical ownership does reside somewhere. But except for our toe-stubbing resident intent on compensation, actual ownership is not apparent, and for the majority does not figure in the apprehension and use of public space. (There are exceptions of course, and much is rightly made of the contended nature of this would-be free domain.) In attempting to engage with this business of public space, we speak of a commodity that ranges from the banal, concrete stuff of place (the domain of our toe-stubber) to a place of spiritual habitation and memory. Such space indeed derives its reality and its energy from this continuing collision of physical habitation and subjective response.

What makes work in this area difficult, as became clear in the work on Five Spaces, is the constant task of redefinition, the continual to and fro between tantalising speculation and candid realism. What is never up for debate is the importance of the attempt, but there is little comfort to be had in occupying this border country between two modes of seeing.

The Five Spaces study has raised many issues around the need for, the nature of, and the nurturing of such spaces. Special places such as these are extremely important, but their very specialness requires that their location, their role, their sustainability (not just physical) have to be justified. Moving beyond these iconic projects, this chapter considers the wider, non-specific terrain of neighbourhoods, which provides the backdrop for these more specialised interventions.

This may seem strange coming from one who has spent a large amount of time in recent years exhorting non-specialists to be aspirational in their dealings with designers. And there is still a frightening mediocrity in the way local environments are designed under the banner of community control. Keeping the flame of design ambition alive is an important part of the challenge and needs careful tending; this is considered in Chapter 6.

This other type of neighbourhood space, the stuff of everyday, needs its own poetry and careful tending but *its* specialness resides in its not being physically assertive. Distinctive and of high quality, effective, yes, but not necessarily important, in the 'look at me' sense.

A NOTE OF CAUTION

Looking back at the depopulated streets of the Five Spaces neighbourhoods, a fundamental question threatens all such agendas (Figs. 5.1, 5.2). Is there a threshold below which it is simply not possible to create good neighbourhood space? Where there just aren't enough people to go around? The phenomenon is visible in today's neighbourhoods, much more than in the urban centres: local shops under pressure, school runs instead of walking, post offices closing, less play outdoors, privatised leisure. These are hard times for the common place. There are powerful forces underlying these local symptoms and these realities cannot be wished away. However, there are encouraging signs that policy is beginning to grasp these contradictions, part of a growing reaction to the impoverishment of civil society. Public space has become the common ground in which everything from transport to health to leisure and recreation policy is finding expression (Fig. 5.3). But it is a huge challenge, and the poorer the population the greater the impact of this diminishment of street life.

Fig. 5.1. Not many people about: traditional shopping streets, preserved with massive housing investment, have lost their urban vitality. Here, Shettleston, in Glasgow's east end

Fig. 5.2. Glasgow, St Vincent Street: here the design of the block gives nothing back to the street in animation or visual enrichment

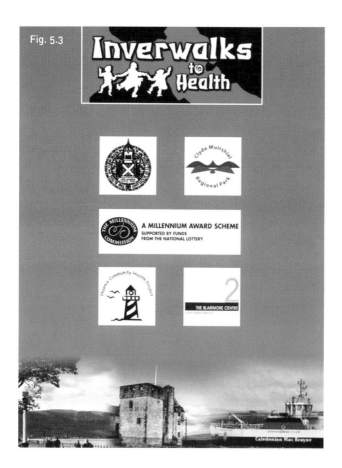

Fig. 5.3

Fig. 5.3. Walking for health: a 'new' way of engaging, spatially and socially. This RIAS (Royal Incorporation of Architects in Scotland) Millennium Award scheme 'You and your environment' produced a spectacular range of personal 'takes' on the built environment

In order to get people back on the streets – this being our base value – new conditions and new reasons for being out have to be found. Street galas, farmers' markets and walk-to-school days may seem contrived (Figs. 5.4, 5.5) but these occasional events at least serve to create a critical mass of people in a given space, bringing a temporary and perhaps memorable experience of communality, of something happening in the 'public room' of a community. Nevertheless, these rare treats cannot substitute for more basic fare – that need to encounter people (even wordlessly) in the world beyond the doorstep. If this potential for encounter is an important dimension of life in the city centre, it is arguably more important in the design of neighbourhoods. We *go to town* for different reasons. Some work there and thus have some access to the frisson of city life. Others may choose the city centre cinema in preference to the multiplex, simply to taste the buzz of a night in town. And, of course there's the shopping experience. Many others, however, rarely visit the centre. Where people live, there will always be the need to engage with the space outside, even if only to buy a pint of milk. There is the possibility that the milk is now bought weekly, and the only local air consumed is that taken between the front door and the car. We are not quite there yet, and in any case it's worth remembering that in areas like the Five Spaces neighbourhoods, car ownership is extremely low[12] [9]. People will always have the need to go out locally. The issue is then the quality of that outdoor experience. People cannot be obliged into this life on the street. That is where creative thought is needed to find ways of bringing the public into the public realm. Doreen Massey [15] makes a similar point:

The public does not already exist as a thing which must be provided for. It must be constituted; it is in a continuous process of being constituted... The challenge is to think what kind of physical space might contribute to that process of constitution.

One argument would be that it is in the experience of what might be called *warm* neighbourhood space that people, especially young people, will learn to situate themselves as citizens. And since, for those deprived of mobility by age, poverty or disability, the neighbourhood provides the primary context, this warmth may be more important than we realise. Warmth (especially in an indifferent climate) may consist of a critical mass of people using a given space at any time, combined with certain physical features that facilitate and enhance the social experience: 'People go where people are,' to quote Gehl [3] again. Katherine Shonfield's powerful cameo comes to mind. Speaking of public space as 'the physical experience of democracy', she continues [16]:

This bodily experience of the random goodwill of the majority, unmediated by hardware, is as fundamental to the experience of humanity as the loving touch of the parent. That loving touch exists in a world beyond language – it is not to be rationalised. Without it we lose our potential to empathise, to respond without defensiveness, we become overly preoccupied with our own edges and borders and we cannot recognise those of other people. The bodily experience of democracy is the social equivalent of this touch: it is the feeling of well-being through which we recognise some of the most important moments of our lifetimes – winning the World Cup, VE Day. These moments give us a temporary sense of membership of a much greater whole; a demos, where status and all other forms of categorisation such as nationality, age and race, are irrelevant.

Fig. 5.4. Farmers' markets revive a tradition lost in Scotland and are expanding rapidly

Fig. 5.4

Fig. 5.5. Glasgow 1999: residents of Royston (and several world monuments) enjoy a day of fiesta in a local space

Shonfield's general definition of public space is helpful, if challenging: 'Public space and time contains every single aspect of urban life that exists beyond home and work'. It moves the emphasis from set-piece provision – the park or square – or lifetime event (the World Cup) to the general quality of the street, the thresholds between one space and another, the public institutions which service the life of these neighbourhoods and the optimisation of these perhaps quite slender materials (Fig. 5.6).

All this seems a long way from the blow-by-blow interrogation of the Five Spaces. The emphasis has shifted, from advocating the creation of little jewels in a desert of mediocrity to a generalised argument for doing something about the overall quality of the public realm. Clearly it's a lot easier, especially in the complicated world of getting things to happen, to identify a single site and do as good a job as possible on it. That need for sparkle, for something special, is worth keeping in mind. New tools are also needed for doing this more commonplace type of neighbourhood work. David Harvey [17] says:

> *There is a politics to place construction ranging... across material, symbolic and representational activities which find its hallmark in the way individuals invest in places and thereby empower themselves collectively by virtue of that investment.*

Fig. 5.6. Barcelona: spontaneous dancing of the Sardana each Saturday evening, an assertion of the democratic ownership of the streets

Fig. 5.6

Chapter 6

Celebrating the mundane: adding cultural value to physical interventions

BEGINNING SOMEWHERE

This piece of work, originally conceived as a straightforward review of a Glasgow 1999 project, has found itself venturing into more complex territory. It has been difficult to begin to do justice to all the themes uncovered along the way; some have only received a sideways glance. However, the city continues to be formed, year by year, and with it the danger of 'provision-led' projects defining the nature of public space (by which is meant the delivery of amenity space on a per capita/hectare basis rather than in a more culturally rooted intention). If the argument of this book is of any value, it is important to suggest a way forward that moves from speculation to real-life delivery.

'FIRST THE LIFE, THEN THE SPACES, THEN THE BUILDINGS' [18]

If agreement is possible on anything, it would surely be on the value of the life-affirming, casual, ordinary encounters associated with life in this part of the public realm – the local neighbourhood. If differing in complexity and texture, this localised public domain is just as much part of Shonfield's 'physical experience of democracy' as the city centre, and is arguably more important in its ubiquity and everyday use. The challenge for designers is to construct the context in which these unspectacular encounters may take place and be further enriched.

Jan Gehl demonstrates again and again the simple precept of understanding how people use a place in order to unlock its potential (surely the designer's role). It is therefore a matter of programme, of bringing people together at certain points. The creation of meaningful space cannot, of course, be reduced to head counts. It is also a qualitative issue – good bus stops, good finishes, a sense of dignity and worth. The endeavour of observation is nevertheless important. The shift is in focus, not simply from place to people, from physical to social, but to people-in-place, social-in-physical. How, then, may this day-to-day reality be explored in a way liable to bring out these latent meanings, networks and memories to enrich the task of place-making?

Cultural work, whether of environmental artists or local history groups, the type of activity which Dolores Hayden [19] describes so well, is an approach favoured by a growing number of projects and was explored to some extent in the Five Spaces. There are risks here. Unless handled very sensitively, this social inclusion-orientated version of the wider culture-led approach to regeneration may seem as contrived as many other participatory mechanisms. A letter in *New Statesman* makes the point most feelingly [20]:

> *On Tyneside, we are submerged by a tide of culture at the moment…Newcastle is not Barcelona – it is beautiful, shitty little Newcastle.*

The writer mentions that the Geordie tradition of dissident socialist republicanism has been completely overlooked in 'third way' chatter about the city's 'great creative potential'.

If the talk here is of cultural work, it will take place in neighbourhoods, ordinary places, and the principle of keeping it simple is important. It will tend to be small scale and relatively modest, with the occasional burst of extravagance. Too rich a cultural mix may be as hard to digest as too 'important' a physical design.

In this resides the basis of a proposal for working on local public space, an agenda that proposes, in the first place, a form of facilitation which has at its core the celebration of local identity, the re-enforcement of delicate networks, the discovery of latent ones, and through that, a heightened apprehension of space and place. In parallel, a process that asks:

- where are the people places in this neighbourhood?
- what kind of activity takes place here?
- how might that be enhanced? (more people, more and different activities, staying longer?)

and proceeds to:

- a physical shopping list that gives clues as to how value may be added to the life of the place, to existing spaces or new ones
- a process of exploration in design, widening the vocabulary of possibility
- an imaginative participatory design process which, eventually, produces a public space strategy.

In a real-life situation this might be expressed in the following strategy.

- Take a small piece of city, and enlist all stakeholders, local and official, in embracing a project to make their place better.
- Find champions for a festival. This would combine celebration of local identity with careful interrogation of the history and potential of the area and would include a preliminary open space audit conducted by local people with professional assistance. (Festival in this sense is taken to mean a focused period of whatever length, with a sense of something special happening.)
- The outputs of the festival would feed into the production of a manifesto, a (multimedia) essay about the nature of the locality, how it works, where it has come from and where it wants to go.
- The open space audit, very light-touch at this stage, would then develop into a public space strategy, combining cultural with spatial ambitions. The document would set down a set of varying and perhaps competing dimensions arising from the festival; ranging from the demand for flowerbeds, to the insight of the artist, to the shortage of playspace, to the disaffection of young people, to the folk memory of industries now disappeared, to the call for a local hero to be recognised. There are well-developed tools for this type of activity in relation to physical space, such as Placecheck, devised by the Urban Design Alliance [21] and Communities in Action [22]. They could easily be expanded to accommodate this cultural activity.

- Having identified ways of accommodating the various ambitions in spatial terms, individual project champions could be sought – council departments, training organisations, the local allotment society, the primary school – and the development and future management of the various spaces negotiated. Funders would presumably warm to this integrated vision. It chimes very neatly with the whole thrust of community planning and budgeting.

- The attraction of this document would be that it would be flexible and would assert its status as a baseline around which further deliberation would necessarily be focused. What it does do, at a crucial point, is establish the primacy of the built environment as the common ground in which lives and policies shape each other.

This scenario is necessarily schematic, but the following are its essential qualities.

- It is comprehensive without being prescriptive.
- It emerges, not from a narrow physical survey, but from an honest attempt to get under the skin of an area.
- It gives equal consideration to the varying claims of citizens to the public space in their neighbourhood, allowing the issue of 'civic' space as we have defined it to be advocated and considered as one of the many ways to create a cohesive place. Starting with flowerpots, we may yet achieve fountains.
- It allows all stakeholders to contract with each other in mutual commitment to the neighbourhood.

The approach advocated here is not entirely new. There is a

stock of examples of culturally-based physical regeneration, a striking example of which – the Royston Road Project – is situated in Glasgow.

THE ROYSTON ROAD PROJECT

Following a successful community campaign in 1999 to see off the demolition of the spire of Royston church in northeast Glasgow, a proposal was developed to make two small parks, one at the foot of the spire and the other in neighbouring Blackhill. A programme of artists' commissions was instituted, specifically designed to allow local people to engage with questions of meaning and identity; who they were, the residents of Royston, in that place and time. There were no physical artworks. Instead there was a local radio station, a rose-naming competition (the growers have delivered the Royston rose 'Where the heart is' to local homes), a Mills and Boon writing workshop, and so on (Figs. 6.1, 6.2).

The parks have now been created and every effort is being made to nurture positive use (Fig. 6.3). Ten local young people have moved into full-time employment, having had training during the construction phase. A publication, video, conference and exhibition at The Lighthouse have established the project as one of the most interesting recent initiatives of its type. It was conceived as taking up the approaches of the Five Spaces project in a less pressured context; the projects shared the same arts commissioning agent who was passionate about the approach pursued. The Royston Road Project is ambitious to connect into the wider issues of housing stock transfer and social and economic regeneration. The team enjoys hard-won respect from the bureaucracies, for the project has delivered on its promise and has won a Scottish Urban Regeneration Award.

It may be said that this is cultural work in a narrower sense than that suggested above, in that it purposely sets the challenge of cultural interrogation in the hands of outsiders,

Fig. 6.1.

Fig. 6.2

Fig. 6.3

Fig. 6.1.   Royston: Bolt fm, a neighbourhood radio station involved young people

Fig. 6.2.   Royston: a writing workshop explored the concept of romance

Fig. 6.3.   Royston: Spire Park, one of two public spaces developed by a local trust. Members are now involved with the development of a community centre

Fig. 6.4. **The Coach House Trust: organic gardening, personal development and community resource**

people whose role it is to make evident to a community the rituals and richness latent in that place.

But no approach should be pre-eminent. If it is the life of a neighbourhood that is being explored, the range of approaches to intervention will be as various as the types of people living there. Some will feel moved to hands-on activity, as the voluntary energy ploughed into garden fetes, school sales and the like has always demonstrated. This should be encouraged. Others, less able to self-start, will be supported in projects designed to teach skills while providing a genuine local service. The Coach House Trust in Glasgow created such a context.

THE COACH HOUSE TRUST

The Coach House Trust, which started life as a project to support skills development for people with a range of problems, undertook work in the back lanes around Belmont Street in Glasgow with the help of a grant from Glasgow 1999. It has grown into a successful social enterprise with an organic nursery, on-site kitchen, recycling facility and small contracting operation, working from a beautifully converted coach house.

The Trust's work has spilled out into the community and is seen as a local resource (Figs. 6.4, 6.5). A community garden

Fig. 6.5

Fig. 6.5. The Coach House Trust: skills development and a good reputation have developed into contracting with local householders

has been created; tucked away behind the shops in the heart of the West End, it offers by turns a place for family celebration and a quiet retreat (Fig. 6.6). The Trust, in common with many such projects, is driven forward by a small team of individuals who have the good sense to combine visionary commitment with the flexibility to allow the organisation, as well as the plants, to grow organically.

There will always be space in this broad approach for that spark of inspiration, the wild card, to be nurtured into something coherent and deliverable. Cranhill Water Tower was one such idea.

CRANHILL WATER TOWER

Glasgow has a ring of water towers, built to serve the vast outer estates of the post-war housing programme. The people of Cranhill obtained a Partnership Fund grant from Glasgow 1999 to do something about their tower, then seen as a local eyesore (Fig. 6.7). The project finally succeeded with the refurbishment and permanent lighting of the tower, in partnership with private, public and community sectors (Fig. 6.8). It has won many awards and featured in the Scottish contribution to the Venice Biennale 2004. Following the success of the Cranhill Water Tower, there was local demand in neighbouring Garthamlock to have *their* towers lit, and a campaign involving the councillor, the community and an artist succeeded in securing funds. These stunning apparitions are now seen by everyone approaching the city from the east, and have become beacons for the area. This in turn has resulted in the inclusion in the city lighting strategy of a ring of such towers in peripheral estates.

Three examples, but many others might be quoted: the steady progress of organisations such as Groundwork, the Greenspace Trusts, British Trust for Conservation Volunteers and other conservation groups in introducing people to the pleasures of collaborative work in the outdoors; the playground projects that engage children and parents in creating stimulating outdoor environments (Fig. 6.9) and, more recently in Scotland, local authority access officers working with local people to assess and plan local paths networks.

Underpinning these is a host of funding and enabling mechanisms, many of which belong to contrasting organisational cultures. From arts council to volunteer bureau, heritage society to safe routes to schools campaign, all are present in the public realm, in both physical and figurative senses. The issue then becomes that of creating an environment in which this rich complex of possibility may become operational.

GOING FORWARD

There remains the question of who will champion an area of work that is so patently fraught with complexities and uncertainties. Is it such a priority anyway? And who will pay? The outlook is far from certain, precisely because of the subject's elusiveness. Housing, schools, health and leisure/play are all substantial and complex pieces of the urban jigsaw, and great effort is being put into delivering these in a physically and socially integrated manner. Something as elusive as public space may seem less pressing.

On the other hand, social inclusion efforts are increasingly understanding the potency of the environment. There is a happy sense of the sustainability agenda beginning to be valued for its complexity and variety; the idea of connectedness being a liberating force, allowing a thousand different flowers to bloom instead of imposing conformity to a standard rootstock of municipal or official breeding. Contradictory challenges confront us: how to connect; maintain vision, direction and accountability; avoid reinventing the wheel while at the same time letting go; encouraging local action, devolving budgets, trusting the people. For this is our

Fig. 6.6.

Fig. 6.6.   The Coach House community garden: many such
gardens are hidden gems; this one is just behind one of the west
end's busiest thoroughfares

current situation – we demand vision at the top but are suspicious of top-down thinking. We encourage local initiative, but realise it lacks the wider view. We see departments committed to the idea of collaboration but finding it difficult to create real-life partnerships and set aside old patterns of thought.

SPACE FOR INNOVATION

Many of the examples in this book, including the Five Spaces, came into being as part of the one-off initiative of the 1999 Festival. Events such as Glasgow 1999 create a space in which such possibilities may emerge. Not only did it provide the platform for a host of approaches, it also created a central point of reference for all the projects and provided a vantage point from which to view their effects and outcomes. But these opportunities do not emerge from nowhere. These high-profile city titles are hotly contested because of the perceived benefits they bring to the city; a powerful agenda accompanies the funding that attaches itself to the winner. They are thus highly political. Other effects – such as that of perspective – are secondary and liable to be missed.

The NESTA fellowship has afforded a privileged space to take advantage of the view from Glasgow 1999. The approach sketched out in this chapter proposes a form of open-ended, hopeful investment in connecting the life of a place to its physical formation. It needs both lightness of touch and driving energy and it needs to be grounded in a fundamental commitment to understanding and responding to people and place – the democratic agenda itself. So the ambition is considerable, arguably no less so than in high-profile, heavily invested events such as Glasgow 1999. To be tested thoroughly, the approach requires a commensurate *ideological* commitment from its champions.

Fig. 6.7

Fig. 6.7. Cranhill Water Tower: before the project, the tower was seen as a problematic eyesore in a very depressed area

Fig. 6.8.

Fig. 6.8. Cranhill Water Tower: the project exceeded its ambitions and has set a precedent for others

Fig. 6.9

Fig. 6.9. School Grounds Improvement Group, Neilston: such projects deliver much bigger gains than their stated agendas

CONCLUSION

The significance of the Five Spaces has to be seen in the overall context of what has been happening in the city and beyond in the years since its inception. Policy thinking has developed, the language of social inclusion has offered more holistic perspectives, and urban renewal and cultural initiatives are increasingly seen as complementary.

At the end of 1999, the Glasgow 1999 Board considered how to ensure a legacy for the achievements of the year. At that time a Public Spaces Trust was proposed to carry forward the issues raised by the Five Spaces and to champion the case for neighbourhood public space in general. For various reasons, this was not pursued. The Greenspace Trust network in Scotland might now provide a vehicle for much of this work, although *grey* as well as *green* issues need to be addressed. The recent and rapid expansion of the development trust movement in Scotland[13] has created a structure that could support deeper change, including community asset ownership and economic development. By implication it confirms the insistence of this book on placing even the most modest spatial intervention within a wider, more critical landscape.

There is no shortage of realism here about the challenges to be faced in the experimental approaches described above, and careful evaluation of these needs to be undertaken before this or any other such project is undertaken. It is one thing to conceptualise the issues; it needs quite another set of skills to make the difference on the ground. But what a difference it could be.

Fig. 7.1.

Fig. 7.1.   Neilston: ecclesiastical outpost, then industrial village, now commuter settlement. The fortunes of this place, in common with many such communities, have always been wedded to urban development

Chapter 7

Postscript: Five Spaces, five years and a new project

It is now five years since the Five Spaces were delivered. In that time their raw newness has worn off and most, for better or worse, have settled down into their neighbourhood landscapes. It has taken that time to be able to form a considered view of the whole, and to speculate on what might have been done differently. Problems have been resolved, or have come to a head; wider moves have created a context for new forms of management and care. What happens in terms of future projects is uncertain, but it is vital that some attempt is made to apply the understanding gained in this work.

Neilston: Space to Live is the real-life experiment that rounds off this voyage into neighbourhood space and it will be the physical and social legacy of the NESTA fellowship. It has not been undertaken lightly. Projects *in the public realm* are just that: interventions with ramifications, in lives and in time, and an individual citizen proposing a substantial initiative has to earn legitimacy. Nonetheless, the lessons learned from the Five Spaces and this study need to be applied with the energy and ambition owed to them, while somehow respecting the modest and everyday textures that define this particular terrain.

Neilston is a dormitory community of around 5000 people, 12 miles from Glasgow centre, but easily accessed by commuter train and motorway. It has its roots in pre-history, mediaeval ecclesiastical settlement and the industrial revolution, being the site of Scotland's second cotton mill in the late 18th century (Fig. 7.1). The last mill closed only in the 1980s. Today, though, Neilston shares much with other neighbourhoods on the urban edges, valued for its community networks and the low-density housing estates favoured by so many (if not by urban designers) (Fig. 7.2). The place is by no means free of social problems. Although no whole wards appear on the scale of most deprived in Scotland, there are significant pockets of quite severe need, with small area profiles within the worst 10 per cent of such areas in Scotland [23]. Its community infrastructure is good, although there is the inevitable pressure on services and facilities from alternatives in nearby Barrhead, Paisley and Glasgow. It has a strong agricultural tradition, but this sector, too, is under stress. This little cameo gives no clear impression of the physical environment, which turns out to be as fragmented as many urban neighbourhoods (Figs. 7.3, 7.4). The natural qualities of its setting, the core village layout and its strong community networks offer the potential for useful and appropriate transformation (Fig. 7.5). In common with so many unassuming places, urban design seems to have passed Neilston by. It is not the piece of city proposed as a testing ground in Chapter 6. However, it presents an interesting challenge and one that may be more typical and potentially significant than urbanists would have us think. As Booth [24], referring to the inception of two departments of suburban studies at Cambridge and Kingston Universities, says:

> *Until last week, the issue of how to understand and build suburbs was a side show compared to the vast industry of urbanists, architecture schools focusing on city centres and city design champions…Given that 84 per cent of the population live in suburban areas, it is a peculiar bias for a profession that declares itself to be driven by the needs of people.*

The same article [24] continues with this contribution (from Sean Griffiths, an architect), timely in respect of anything that might be attempted in the Neilston situation, but also vindication of the lessons of the Five Spaces:

> *The last thing the suburbs need is a bunch of architects coming in and having a vision…There is a danger that architects will just import a set of urban renaissance values – visions of public space and attempts to introduce visual coherence and architectural order to something that is much more complex.*

Fig. 7.2

Fig. 7.2. Housing estates set the development
agenda for countless suburban neighbourhoods

The article addresses the fact that in order to fulfil the housing targets for the coming century, new suburbs, even whole new settlements, will inevitably be built. But the point could just as easily be made of the countless existing neighbourhoods experiencing the challenge of changed circumstances, themselves the casualties, perhaps, of the sparkling diversions thrown up by centres of the new urbanity. Dr Vesna Goldsworthy of the Department of Urban Studies at Kingston University points to the way in which communities have shaped suburbia over time, and acknowledges the challenge of designing social spaces for these situations [24]:

> *I am not sure we really have an idea of what works because what works as an architectural model often becomes windswept and bleak...It's about the willingness of people to make the suburbs the centre of their lives.*

No solutions, then, but a welcome corroboration of the thrust of this book.

NEILSTON: SPACE TO LIVE – A SNAPSHOT

The method set out in Chapter 6 was followed closely in the initiation of this project, which proposed the dual strands of *Life* and *Space* as its central components. Despite some initial difficulty in communicating the concept (dog-fouling and litter not seeming to need such an exalted prospectus), the project is now up and running, with a large management committee and a considerable degree of support from the local authority (East Renfrewshire Council). After well-attended inaugural meetings, the project had its first real outing at the annual agricultural show, itself a cherished tradition of Neilston life (Fig. 7.6).

The project is working towards the delivery of a festival (Neilston Live) in Summer 2005, with a parallel process establishing the spatial context. The 'Big Do' in late 2005 will build on the energy and networks created or consolidated in the development of the festival. Plans are already in hand to collaborate with a range of council officers whose programmes are directed towards community planning goals

Fig. 7.3

Fig. 7.4

Fig. 7.3. Neilston Main Street: the shops survive, though more limited in range than in previous years. The urban fabric is unsightly and incoherent, relieved by a few historic fragments

Fig. 7.4. Neilston Main Street: valuable public facilities float in undifferentiated open space and suffer much vandalism as a result

Fig. 7.5. The Neilston Show: prize animals, tug-o-war, school races — attractions indeed, but surpassed, one suspects, in the gentle pleasure of meeting and greeting

Fig. 7.5

that sit very well with the cross-cutting scope of the project.

It is hoped that artists will be central to the process, not necessarily in the front line of design teams but in a much looser relationship to the Life side of the equation. For it is in the insights of well-chosen and socially engaged artists that rich and perhaps overlooked aspects of the common place can be revealed. If the recent invocation of arts (especially the visual arts) as a salve to the manifest ills of space creation has been found wanting, there is the danger that its most powerful contribution is overlooked. Stuart MacDonald (director of The Lighthouse, Scotland's Centre for Architecture, Design and the City) has said [25]:

> *The power of art lies in its otherness, its ability to defy logic, to subvert, to symbolise, to create metaphor, to vacillate, to dilly-dally.*

Stuart MacDonald asserts that it is not the arts, but design, properly understood and applied with all the subtlety and understanding that should characterise it, which is the proper competence for the delivery of good environments, and the distinction is worth making. The argument is that, at this point, there is insufficient general understanding of 'nothing special' places to hand a designer an adequate brief. Their complexity is belied by their pedestrian demeanour, and the artist's presence, with independence of action, provokes response, encourages reflection and creates intellectual context where perhaps there had seemed to be a void. Direct engagement with residents or particular groups may be part of the practice, or not; in both cases something changes. (Figs. 7.7–7.9).

So the attempt is made: the Life and the Spaces. Perhaps the links drawn between space and life will be seen to work at the conceptual but not at the operational level. Perhaps the ambition for a strategy attempts to impose the tactics of the masterplan to the organic evolution of the suburb. Perhaps everyday spaces should be left to their essential ordinariness.

Time will tell.

Fig. 7.6.

Fig. 7.6. Neilston: Space to Live—residents take a first step towards engagement at the Neilston Show

Fig. 7.7

Fig. 7.7. The Royston project: as part of the artists' programme, Stephen Healy chose to create a series of large-format photographic portraits of the dog-walkers of the area. Invoking the tradition of heroic portraiture, the work renders remarkable the unremarkable life of the street, and the individuality of local residents. More important, people loved it

Fig. 7.8. Ceremonial for Springburn Public Halls, May 1999: artists Dan Dubowitz and Matt Baker of Heisenberg transformed the facade of the listed but derelict public halls. Candles, live music and a glorious sunset created a magical event, evoking its past life and inspiring questions about its future

Fig. 7.9. Springburn: fond memories of 'the dancing' produce spontaneous —and moving—habitation of the 'public room' of the street

NOTES

1   Glasgow, UK City of Architecture and Design 1999, a title awarded by the Arts Council (subsequently the Arts Council of England), as the last of the year-long celebrations of the arts, culminating in 2000 with the Year of the Artist.

2   It is interesting, with hindsight, to ask why Barcelona, Mediterranean in culture and climate, was singled out as an exemplar. Certainly it is much loved by designers and much admired for its municipal vision. However, it has arguably less in common with Glasgow than other more northerly cities with whom our relationship with the outdoors is more comparable.

3   Scottish Homes (now Communities Scotland) had a similar remit to the Housing Corporation in England.

4   NESTA, the National Endowment for Science, Technology and the Arts (www.nesta.org.uk).

5   Transcripts of the interviews are held by the author.

6   Design's on You: design education courses and European study tours delivered by SHARE for housing association committee members.

7   Students at the Department of Geography, Glasgow University carried out street surveys of local reaction.

8   Molendinar Park Housing Association received RIBA Client of the Year 2001 – the only housing organisation ever to receive the award.

9   The Lighthouse, Scotland's Centre for Architecture, Design and the City (www.thelighthouse.co.uk).

10 On-street research at the time of the Five Spaces' completion by geography students at Glasgow University revealed such a spectrum.

11 Difficult to define, it is sometimes called 'grey' space, and would include squares, pedestrian areas, and the pieces of hard landscaping that are increasingly employed to create the new urban realm that graces many city centres. It is used here to call into focus all public space that is not green, and specifically, in this chapter, that which may be considered special or civic in its ambition.

12 Car ownership in Glasgow (in 2000) was 246 per 1000, representing 61% of the UK average. In poor areas, the figure is much lower.

13 www.dtascot.org.uk

REFERENCES

[1] LACK J. (ed.) *Five Spaces: New Urban Landscapes for Glasgow.* Glasgow 1999/August Media, London, 1999 (available from The Lighthouse, Tel: 0141 221 6362, email: info@thelighthouse.co.uk).

[2] ALEXANDER C. *et al. A Pattern Language: Towns, Buildings, Construction.* Oxford University Press, New York, 1977.

[3] GEHL J. *Life Between Buildings, 4th edn.* Danish Architectural Press, Copenhagen, 2001.

[4] LYNCH K. *The Image of the City.* MIT Press, Cambridge, MA, 1960.

[5] JACOBS J. *The Death and Life of Great American Cities.* Random House, New York, 1961.

[6] WORPOLE K. *People, Parks and Cities.* HMSO, London, 1996.

[7] PUTHOD C. *et al. Creative Spaces: A Toolkit for Participatory Urban Design.* Architecture Foundation, London, 2000.

[8] GLASGOW CITY COUNCIL. *Glasgow, City of Light.* GCC, Glasgow, 2002.

[9] GLASGOW CITY COUNCIL. *2020 Vision.* Dept. of Land Services, GCC, Glasgow, 2001.

[10] DTLR. *Green Spaces, Better Places.* Final report of Urban Green Spaces Task Force, London, 2002.

[11] SCOTTISH EXECUTIVE. *Designing Places.* Scottish Executive, Edinburgh, 2001.

[12] SENNET R. *The Conscience of the Eye: The Design and Social Life of Cities.* Knopf, New York, 1991.

[13] MCKENZIE R. *Public Sculpture of Glasgow.* Liverpool University Press, Liverpool, 2002, p. xiv.

[14] LOBELL J. *Between Silence and Light: Spirit in the Architecture of Louis Kahn.* Shambhala Publications, Boulder, CO, 1979.

[15] MASSEY D. Public conscience. *Building Design*, May 23, 2003, p. 32.

[16] SHONFIELD K. At home with strangers. *The Richness of Cities.* Comedia and Demos, London, 1999, working paper 8, p. 9.

[17] HARVEY D. From space to place and back again. In *The Power of Place: Urban Landscapes as Public History* (HAYDEN D. (ed.)). MIT Press, Cambridge, MA, 1995.

[18] GEHL J. *Creating a Human Quality in the City.* Lecture, Royal Danish Academy of Fine Arts, School of Architecture, March 2003.

[19] HAYDEN D. *The Power of Place: Urban Landscapes as Public History.* MIT Press, Cambridge, MA, 1995.

[20] ARMSTRONG K. Letter. *New Statesman*, May 26, 2003, p. 38.

[21] URBAN DESIGN ALLIANCE. *Placecheck.* UDAL, London, 2002.

[22] ROMICE O. and FREY H. *Communities in Action: The Handbook.* University of Strathclyde, 2003.

[23] SCOTTISH EXECUTIVE. *Scottish Index of Deprivation 2004,* Scottish Executive, Edinburgh, 2004 and East Renfrewshire Community Planning Partnership, *Socioeconomic Profile,* 2004.

[24] BOOTH R. The 'burbs bite back. *Building Design*, April 30, 2004, p. 9.

[25] MACDONALD S. *Patronising Places.* A response to First Minister Jack McConnell's St Andrew's Day Speech 2003. Macmag 29, Mackintosh School of Architecture, Glasgow, 2004.

BIBLIOGRAPHY

ALEXANDER C. *et al*. *A Pattern Language: Towns, Buildings, Construction*. Oxford University Press, New York, 1977.

BANKSIDE OPEN SPACES TRUST. *In My Backyard: Creating a Sense of Place in Bankside*. BOST, London, 2002.

BATH & NORTH-EAST SOMERSET COUNCIL. *Life in the Public Realm: A Rationale*. B&NESC, Bath, 2002.

BENN M. Livelihood: work in the new urban economy. *The Richness of Cities*. Comedia and Demos, London, 1999, working paper 6.

BILLINGHAM J. and COLE R. *The Good Place Guide*. Batsford, London, 2002.

BOOTH R. The 'burbs bite back. *Building Design*, April 30, 2004.

BORDEN I. *et al*. (eds) *Strangely Familiar: Narratives of Architecture in the City*. Routledge, London, 1996.

BORDEN I. *et al. The Unknown City: Contesting Architecture and Social Space.* MIT Press, Cambridge, MA, 2001.

BROADBENT G. *Emerging Concepts in Urban Space Design*. E&FN Spon, London, 1990.

CABE SPACE. *Manifesto for Better Public Spaces*. Cabe, London, 2004.

CABE SPACE. *What Would You do With This Space? Involving Young People in the Care and Design of Urban Spaces.* Cabe, London, 2004.

CALCUTT J. Rack and ruin; artists and regeneration in Glasgow's 5 Spaces. *Sculpture Matters, Scottish Sculpture Trust*, 2002, No. 15.

CARA S. *et al*. The learning city in the learning age. *The Richness of Cities*. Comedia and Demos, London, 1999, working paper 10.

CHRISTIE I. and WORPOLE K. *Changing Places, Changing Lives*: Seizing the Challenge of Environmental Modernisation and *Social Inclusion*. Groundwork, Birmingham, 2000.

COIN STREET COMMUNITY BUILDERS. *There is Another Way*. CSCB, London, 2003.

COWAN R. *The Connected City*. Urban Initiatives, London, 1997.

DAWES M. and GUEST A. Barcelona comes to Glasgow: a new direction for collaborative practice? *Sculpture Matters, Scottish Sculpture Trust*, 1999, No. 6.

DEVELOPMENT TRUST ASSOCIATION. *Fabulous Beasts: Stories of Community Enterprise from the DTA*. DTS, London, 2002.

DEPARTMENT FOR TRANSPORT, LOCAL GOVERNMENT AND THE REGIONS. *Green Spaces, Better Places*. Final report of Urban Green Spaces Task Force, London, 2002.

DUNNET N. *et al. Improving Urban Parks Play Areas and Urban Green Spaces*. ODPM, London, 2002.

GARDINER L. *et al. Royston Road Parks.* The Centre on behalf of the Royston Road Project, Glasgow, 2002.

GEHL J. *Life Between Buildings*, 4th edn. Danish Architectural Press, Copenhagen, 2001.

GEHL J. and GEMZØE L. *Public Spaces, Public Life*. Danish Architectural Press, Copenhagen, 1996.

GEHL J. and GEMZØE L. *New City Spaces.* Danish Architectural Press, Copenhagen, 2000.

GLASGOW CITY COUNCIL. *2020 VISION: Draft for Consultation.* GCC Land Services Dept., Glasgow, 2001.

GLASGOW CITY COUNCIL. *Glasgow City of Light*. GCC, Glasgow, 2002.

GLASGOW CITY COUNCIL. *Connecting Glasgow: the Glasgow Access and Walking Strategy.* GCC, Glasgow, 2003.

GLASGOW CITY COUNCIL. *Strategic Review of Parks and Open Spaces Public Consultation.* GCC Land Services Dept., Glasgow, 2004.

GLASGOW CITY COUNCIL. *Environment Strategy*. GCC, Glasgow, 1998.

GLASGOW WORKS AND ROCK SPECIAL PROJECTS. *Environmental Awareness Report: Raising Awareness of Environmental Dereliction in Glasgow*, GWRSP, Glasgow, 2000.

GLENDINNING M. and PAGE D. *Clone City: Crisis and Renewal in Contemporary Scottish Architecture.* Polygon, Edinburgh, 1999.

GREATER LONDON AUTHORITY. *Making Space for Londoners*. GLA, London, 2002.

GREENHALGH L. *et al.* New departures. *The Richness of Cities.* Comedia and Demos, London, 1999, working paper 1.

GREENHALGH L. Habitat: reconnecting housing to city policy. *The Richness of Cities.* Comedia and Demos, London, 1999, working paper 5.

GREENSPACE SCOTLAND. *Strategy 2002–2005*. Greenspace, Stirling, 2002.

GUEST A. and McKENZIE R. *Dangerous Ground: Sculpture in the City.* Scottish Sculpture Trust, Edinburgh, 1999.

HAMPSHIRE COUNTY COUNCIL. *In Suburbia.* HCC Environment Dept., Winchester, 2002.

HARDING D. *Meanwhile Artist* and other essays on socially engaged art practice. 2003 (www.davidharding.org/articles).

HARDING D. and GUEST A. (eds) *The City is a Work of Art*. Scottish Sculpture Trust, Stirling, 1994.

HAYDEN D. *The Power of Place: Urban Landscapes as Public History.* MIT Press, Cambridge, MA, 1995.

JACOBS J. *The Death and Life of Great American Cities*. Random House, New York, 1961.

JENKINS D. Partnerships and power; leadership and accountability in urban governance. *The Richness of Cities.* Comedia and Demos, London, 1999, working paper 4.

Kearns A. and Parkinson M. The significance of neighbourhood. *Urban Studies*, 2001, No. 38.

Kit Campbell Assocs. *Rethinking Open Space: Open Space Provision and Management – A Way Forward*. Scottish Executive Central Research Unit, Edinburgh, 2001.

Lack J. (ed.) *Five Spaces*: *New Urban Landscapes for Glasgow*. Glasgow 1999/August Media, London, 1999.

Landry C. *The Creative City.* Earthscan, London, 2000.

Landry C. *et al. The Art of Regeneration: Urban Renewal Through Cultural Activity*. Comedia and Demos, London, 1996.

Lefebvre H. *The Production of Space.* Blackwell, Malden, 1991.

Legates R. T. and Stout F. *The City Reader.* Routledge, London, 1996.

Levett R. and Christie I. Towards the ecopolis: sustainable development and urban governance. *The Richness of Cities.* Comedia and Demos, London, 1999, working paper 12.

Lighthouse. *Common-place*. The Lighthouse, Glasgow, 2003.

Lighthouse. *Fieldtrip*. The Lighthouse, Glasgow, 2004.

Llewellyn-Davies. *Urban Design Compendium*. English Partnerships, London, 2000.

Lobell J. *Between Silence and Light: Spirit in the Architecture of Louis Kahn.* Shambhala Publications, Boulder, CO, 1979.

Lynch K. *The Image of the City.* MIT Press, Cambridge, MA, 1960.

MacDonald S. *Patronising Places.* A response to First Minister Jack McConnell's St Andrew's Day Speech 2003. Macmag 29, Mackintosh School of Architecture, Glasgow, 2004.

Massey D. Public Conscience. *Building Design*, May 23, 2003, p. 32.

McKenzie R. *Public Sculpture of Glasgow.* Liverpool University Press, Liverpool, 2002.

Miles M. and Kirkham, N. (eds) *Cultures and Settlements*. Intellect, Bristol, 2003.

Office of the Deputy Prime Minister. *Living Places: Cleaner, Safer, Greener.* ODPM, London, 2002.

Puthod C. *et al. Creative Spaces: A Toolkit for Participatory Urban Design*. Architecture Foundation, London, 2000.

Rogers R. *Towards An Urban Renaissance: Final Report of the Urban Task Force.* Spon, London,1999.

Romice O. and Frey H. *Communities in Action: The Handbook.* University of Strathclyde, 2003.

Schwartz A. (ed.) *How to Turn a Place Around: A Handbook for Creating Successful Public Spaces*. PPS Inc., New York, 2001.

Scottish Executive. *Creating Our Future…Minding Our Past*. Scottish Executive, Edinburgh, 2000.

Scottish Executive. *A Policy on Architecture for Scotland.* Scottish Executive, Edinburgh, 2001.

SCOTTISH EXECUTIVE. *Designing Places.* Scottish Executive, Edinburgh, 2001.

SCOTTISH EXECUTIVE. *Design Statements (PAN 68).* Scottish Executive, Edinburgh, 2003.

SCOTTISH EXECUTIVE. *Planning and Open Space (PAN 65).* Scottish Executive, Edinburgh, 2003.

SCOTTISH EXECUTIVE. *Scottish Index of Deprivation.* Scottish Executive, Edinburgh, 2003,.

SELMAN P. *Local Sustainability.* Paul Chapman, London, 1996.

SENNET R. *The Conscience of the Eye: The Design and Social Life of Cities.* Knopf, New York, 1991.

SHONFIELD K. At home with strangers. *The Richness of Cities.* Comedia and Demos, London, 1999, working paper 8.

SOLESBURY W. Good connections: helping people to communicate in cities. *The Richness of Cities.* Comedia and Demos, London, 1999, working paper 9.

URBAN DESIGN ALLIANCE. *Placecheck.* UDAL, London, 2002.

WARD C. *The Child in the City.* Architectural Press, London, 1978.

WARD THOMPSON K. Urban open space in the 21st century. *Landscape and Urban Planning*, 2002, 60, pp. 59-72.

WATES N. *The Community Planning Handbook.* Earthscan, London, 1999.

WORPOLE K. *People, Parks and Cities.* HMSO, London, 1996.

WORPOLE K. Nothing to fear? Trust and respect in urban communities. *The Richness of Cities.* Comedia and Demos, London, 1999, working paper 2.

WORPOLE K. *Here Comes the Sun: Architecture and Public Space in 20th Century European Culture.* Reaktion, London, 2000.

WORPOLE K. *In Our Backyard: The Social Promise of Environmentalism.* Green Alliance, London, 2000.

WORPOLE K. *People and Spaces.* Urban Green Spaces Task Force, Working Group 3, DTLR, London, 2002.

WORPOLE K. *No Particular Place to Go? Children, Young People and Public Space.* Groundwork, Birmingham, 2003.

WORPOLE K. and CHRISTIE I. *Changing Places, Changing Lives.* Groundwork UK, Birmingham, 1999.

WORPOLE K. and GREENHALGH L. *Park Life: Urban Parks & Social Renewal.* Comedia and Demos, London, 1995.

WORPOLE K. and GREENHALGH L. *The Freedom of the City.* Comedia and Demos, London, 1996.

WORPOLE K. and GREENHALGH L. *The Richness of Cities.* Comedia and Demos, London, 1999, final report.

URBAN DESIGN GROUP

Founded in 1978, the Urban Design Group (UDG) is a campaigning membership organisation. Its aims are to:

- Promote best practice in urban design.
- Build an effective framework of policy in local and central government.
- Improve urban design skills.
- Promote collaboration in the urban design process.

Membership starts at just £40 a year for individuals. That includes a subscription to *Urban Design*, the leading quarterly journal in its field, and discounts on UDG events in the UK and study tours abroad. There are additional categories of membership for local authorities, urban design practices, students, libraries and universities, with further discounts for training and recruitment. STREET is the UDG's young urban designers' network.

Email admin@udg.org.uk for further information or visit our website www.udg.org.uk.

Urban Design Group
70 Cowcross Street
London EC1M 6EJ

Urban Design Group
Membership Application Form

May we include these details in the UDG Sourcebook
(available to members; on sale; and displayed on the UDG website)?

Name ☐ Yes ☐ No

Delivery address

Postcode ☐ Yes ☐ No

Telephone ☐ Yes ☐ No

Mobile ☐ Yes ☐ No

Fax ☐ Yes ☐ No

Email ☐ Yes ☐ No

Billing address (if different)

Course/Year (students only)

Current membership of professional institutes

Employer's name

Address

Postcode

Telephone

Email

Indicate the region to which you wish to be affiliated (tick one only):

East Midlands ☐ West Midlands ☐ East Anglia ☐ North ☐
North East ☐ North West ☐ South West ☐ South ☐
Yorkshire ☐ London and SE ☐ Scotland ☐ Wales ☐
Northern Ireland ☐ Outside UK ☐

Please tick membership category

☐ Individual £40
☐ Student/Concession £20 (UK only)
☐ Library £40
☐ Local authority £100 (includes two copies of UDQ)
☐ Practice £250 (includes entries in UDQ Practice Index and Sourcebook, and listing on website)

Tick here if you do not want to receive mailings of job adverts ☐

Paying your subscription by standing order is a great help to the UDG

Details for Standing Order Mandate
(to be sent to UDG)

To (name of bank)

Bank address

Bank postcode

Bank sort code

Please pay Natwest, 68 Church Street, Lancaster LA1 1LN
(Sort Code 01 54 90)
For the credit of the Urban Design Group
(account number 89621271)

The sum of £

Amount in words

Account name

Account number

Commencing

and then every 12 months

Or send a cheque payable to: Urban Design Group

Return your completed application to:

Urban Design Group
70 Cowcross Street, London EC1M 6EJ
Tel: 020 7250 0892
Fax: 020 7250 0872
admin@udg.org.uk

Signed   Date

Gift Aid declaration As a registered charity the UDG can reclaim tax on your annual subscription through the Gift Aid scheme – as long as you are a taxpayer and pay an amount of income tax or capital gains tax at least equal to the tax we reclaim (currently 28p for each £1 you give). Please sign the declaration below if you are a taxpayer. It will not cost you anything, but the UDG will receive from the Inland Revenue tax you have already paid.
I wish the Urban Design Group to treat as Gift Aid all membership subscriptions I have paid on or after the date of this declaration.

Signed   Date

You can cancel this declaration at any time by contacting the Urban Design Group.

INDEX

Note: Page numbers in red refer to
photographs.